Gleanings of Grace
Stories Depicting My Journey into Joy

THEA COKER

Trysting Place
Fort Myers, Florida

Gleanings of Grace: Stories Depicting My Journey into Joy
First Edition, 2017
Copyright © 2017 Thea Coker

Publisher
Trysting Place
1605 Hendry St.
Fort Myers, FL 33901
(850) 221-4549

ISBN: 978-0-692-92983-4 (Print)
ISBN: 978-0-692-92984-1 (e-readers)

Project Manager: Marla Markman, MarlaMarkman.com
Cover Design: Slant Partners, SlantPartners.com
Interior Design: Andrew Chapman, SocialMotionPublishing.com

Printed in the United States of America
21 20 19 18 17 / 10 9 8 7 6 5 4 3 2 1

*To my mother, Jo Burge, the first voice that ever told me
Jesus loved me. I am forever grateful!*

CONTENTS

ACKNOWLEDGEMENTS

MY MAMA TAUGHT me to say, "Thank you." Every time I was given something, she would say, "Thea, now what do you say?" I eventually learned that the proper response was, of course, "Thank you." My mama was teaching me good manners!

God taught me to say "thank you" for all things.

My book is just Mama's little girl learning to say "thank you" to the Sovereign God who deserves to be praised forever and ever.

This book was birthed in my heart years before I ever wrote a word. I never really set out to write a book, but I felt compelled to put words to the beautiful and personal touches of the grace of God to me. Eventually, words began to flow through my mind and spill onto pages, and so these stories were birthed. But so many have helped me along the way.

First, to my Lord and Master, Jesus Christ, and my sweet little mother, Jo Burge, who first told me about Him and then showed me what He looked like. I am forever grateful.

Second, to my loving husband and retired pastor, Don Coker. You have shown me, in many ways, what real love looks like. Thank you for encouraging me to write and for all your proofreading to be sure I was theologically sound.

Third, to our eldest son and daughter in law, Phil and Angela Fischler. Each time I wrote a new story, they listened intently, sometimes crying, and said, "Mom, other people need to hear these too." They took the ball and ran with it, getting my stories published. They were the loving hands that carried my dream to fruition.

To all our other "kids" for their constant love and encouragement: Jason, Jeff and Kandace; Jermel and Heidi; Ben and Gretchen; and our 17 grandchildren. Thank you for letting me love you and pray for you. You are precious treasures.

And to my many friends who have lived life with me, prayed with me and for me, and are always encouraging me along this journey, thank you.

Finally, to the team who put my book to flight, thank you all!

FOREWORD

RECENTLY, WHILE FINISHING up a class at one of Tennessee's state prisons, an inmate observed that he had always been told to use his head. He said that while he did do this, nothing was ever put in his head that was of value, thus leading to his demise and imprisonment. Thea Coker's book, on the other hand, will give something of great value to help anyone walk in God's ways.

While sitting early one morning, sipping coffee and listening to a few stories that Thea had written, I was both blessed and encouraged. It was like meeting other followers of Jesus Christ, though not in a physical sense, but through Thea's words about them. Her words clearly encapsulated those followers she wrote about. I wholeheartedly endorse these stories from Thea Coker. You, too, will be encouraged and challenged by this book. Some books are good to read, others are important to read, but few demand to be read. This book falls into the latter group. The reason is that this book shares real character-building stories about real people. It is a good daily devotional for any family, enabling them to make observations about the Christian character.

Dr. Gale Hartley
Pastor, Bethany Baptist Church
Mountain City, Tennessee

Introduction

HI! MY NAME is Thea Judith Burge.

I am 3 years old and my mama said, "Thea Judith, you've got a lot to learn!"

In time, I did! I now live "to declare the goodness of the Lord in the land of the living!"

The following 52 stories are true stories from my life. They are based on personal experiences or at least developed from a seed thought of a memory I had as a small child.

I'm old now and people often comment after reading one of my "little girl" stories, "How can you remember all those details?" My answer: "I can't!" A faint memory comes to me, like a burst of light, a single experience remembered by a feeling or a smell or an old yellowing photo. And from those memories, the stories unfold of the chubby little tan girl named Thea!

I wanted to write them down before I forget them, as all old people do, before those sweet memories are gone forever. As we age, forgetfulness happens to us all. You're young, and then, if fortunate, you're old, and then you die and your experiences die off with you. That's just life!

As I wrote these little stories, they were being written by an older woman looking at her younger self through "spectacles of grace." I am kinder to myself now that I'm older, only because I've known God longer through His Word, the Bible. I know Him to be full of loving-kindness and tender mercies that He lavishes on His children. I love it, and I love Him, and can't thank Him enough for what He's done to me, in me, for me and through me!

After sharing my stories with a few friends, I realized that everyone has these same feelings at times in their lives! The feelings of doubt, anger, insecurity, loneliness, fear, worry and also pride, blame, self-sufficiency, self-exaltation and the "I'm the boss of me" place in the center of our heart affects us all. These feelings we try so hard to control, in reality, can only be overcome by a greater power than we have in ourselves. It is the only power that can really change a person: the power of the love of God, revealed in the sacrificial love and life, death and resurrection of His only begotten Son, the Messiah, our Savior, the Lord Jesus Christ! Immanuel, God with us!

All I can hope to do with these little stories is tempt you to go further than where you are in your knowledge of God, which is mainly done through reading the Bible, seeing Him in His creation and spending time in prayer and surrender. He promises we will find Him if we seek Him with all our heart. I'll let you in on a little secret: You will never seek Him unless He seeks you first. God is always the initiator … we can only respond!

I hope you do respond to Him. If you find yourself drawn into these stories in some small way, just BE there with me and look for God around you. His voice may also be calling you as Jesus called to His disciples: "Come, follow me!"

"Come unto Me, all you that labor and are heaven laden, and I will give you rest. Take My yoke upon you, and learn of Me; for I am meek and lowly in heart; and you will find rest for your soul" (Matthew 11:28-30).

Getting the Most Out of This Book

1. What is the Big Idea of this story?
2. Has anything like this ever happened to you or does it remind you of anything?
3. How did this story make you feel? Did it cause you to think differently about anything?
4. Did the scriptures used in this chapter speak to you?
5. What, if any, principles or applications can you take away from this story that you can apply in your life or share?

1
The Gleaners

"And she went, and came, and gleaned in the field after the reapers: and her hap was to light on a part of the field belonging to Boaz" *(Ruth 2:3).*

GLEANERS, THAT'S A word we don't use much anymore. Gleaners were those who were poverty-stricken, the poor ones, the ones with nothing to eat, hungry and searching for food. Gleaners followed the ones of wealth. Gleaners went out to the field to perform the menial task of gathering whatever was left behind. They ate the leftovers after the landowners had finished harvesting their crops. Their hunger was satisfied by the scraps of the rich.

I am a gleaner, not in the sense of its original definition of course, but in a broad sense, I have been satisfied by leftovers of those owners of great wealth. Not material wealth, but wealth far greater than what mere money can buy: spiritual wealth. My parents left it to me.

My parents were charter members of the Warrington Presbyterian Church. It was founded in the mid '40s a few years after the Great Depression. A handful of meager young Christians, wanting to serve the Lord together in their community, began meeting in a local elementary school.

In time, the church began to grow. These young Christians, so eager to serve the Lord, moved around the corner and found a home in a metal military Quonset hut. The Lord had so destined that church to be situated close to a naval base, Pensacola Naval Air station, affectionately known by area locals as the home of the Blue Angels! Most people recognize the Blue Angels as the fantastic daredevil jet planes flown only by an elite few naval pilots.

Since the naval air station was so close to the church, it became a reservoir of diverse people from all over the world. There was a constant flow of new people as the Navy moved its population around the world, and Warrington Presbyterian Church was just a stop on their military journey! It had a very small start but soon began to grow with the rapid influx of families and students moving in and out of Pensacola, Florida.

There was a small core group of people who made up the Warrington Presbyterian Church; my parents were part of that core. I remember when it was a very small group of families meeting in the old metal Quonset hut. In the summer with no air conditioning, it was like an oven! There were big brown fans on the floor with round whirling blades, giving a humming noise to the background. We relentlessly fanned ourselves using little round cardboard paper fans on a stick that were furnished to us by the local funeral parlor.

The large room of the Quonset hut was portioned off by wooden dividers for the individual Sunday school classes. Each little class had a small wooden table with a few chairs and sometimes a flannel graft board sitting on an easel, which was used to help the teacher explain the Bible stories. She would let us stick the Bible character cutouts on the flannel board. Sitting on a little wooden chair in the sweltering heat, I first began to learn about the Bible. It was there I learned about God, our Heavenly Father, about Jesus, His only Son our Savior, and the Holy Spirit who lived inside us after we became Christians. Each week I was taught the Bible and how God worked in the lives of people. That's where I met Adam and Eve, David and Goliath, Samson and Delilah, John the Baptist, and Jesus and His disciples. That's where I learned the true meaning of Christmas and Easter. Sitting on a little wooden chair, having red Kool-Aid and graham cracker snacks, I was taught about God and those who lived before me. I was taught how I was to conduct myself with all the commandments God left us in the Bible.

As far back as I can remember, I have considered myself a Christian. My parents were Christian, I went to a Christian church, they read the Christian Bible, and certainly I was Christian. Most everyone I knew back then went to some sort of Christian church. In my small mind, I really thought everyone was a Christian and only the wicked people who did bad things were not Christian. Being Christian was almost like my nationality, like being German or Spanish. I was Christian.

I learned many good and useful things in that little church and I thank God for all the Sunday school teachers and Bible school teachers I had throughout the years, but it did not make me a Christian. That is not where I really began to see Jesus. I saw Jesus in my mother and my father, but mostly in my mother's heart and her intimate love relationship with the

Lord and His Holy Word.

My entire life she began each day, very early in the morning before anyone was up, on her knees, in His Word, surrendering all to Him, allowing her own famished heart to be renewed by His Word. By being in His Word each morning, God filled my mother with His love and peace, and then she rose to let His love spill out to others. I was one of the others. But for many years, I was not easy to love.

As I sit here thinking about my life as a little girl growing up in Beach Haven, a little subculture of Pensacola, Florida, I am so grateful to God. I was loved by two middle-aged parents who were true Christians by the time I arrived on the scene of their lives. We did not have a lot of material blessings but always enough of what we truly needed.

I grew up in a time of freedom in America. My early childhood was pretty much happy and peaceful. We lived in a small house near the beach with lots of wooded area nearby, which kept me busy with my neighbor buddies for hours on end. It was fun and a great place to grow up. Many of the stories I have written about were seeded in those memories from my childhood in Beach Haven.

As an older woman looking back on that little girl, so much of the fruit of faith that I hold so precious now was gleaned from the active working of faith in my parents' lives. I reaped the leftovers of their harvest. I have gleaned nourishment from their lives of faithful service to the Lord … and I am gleaning still.

Fast-forward to the present. My husband recently retired from the pastorate after 33 years in ministry, and I also recently retired from working 35 years in a dental practice. Now what?

How much time do I have left on this earth, and what do I spend my time doing?

Perhaps my children or my grandchildren might want to glean from my life of faith one day. I ask myself during my quiet times, "Thea, is there anything worth gleaning from your life?"

I have always loved to read and write stories. My kids love them, so I decided to begin writing stories from my own past and lessons I have learned along the way. Perhaps they too will become "gleaners" from a woman who has loved them immensely, although imperfectly, but has learned to sit at the feet of Jesus and listen to His Word.

"Taste and see that the Lord is good" (Psalm 34:8).

Leaving spiritual truths for you, my children, can be like eating delicious, luscious fruit when you are famished. I pray that you, my children and grandchildren (and perhaps others along the way), will take and eat and be refreshed as you see Jesus in these moments with me.

"So we, Your people and the sheep of Your pasture will give thanks to You forever; to all generations we will tell of Your praise" (Psalm 79:13).

"Blessed is the man who trusts in the Lord, and whose hope is in the Lord. For He shall be like a tree planted by the waters, which spread out it roots by the river and will not fear when heat comes but its leaf will be green and will not be anxious in the year of drought, nor will cease from yielding fruit" (Jeremiah 17:7-8).

2
"Sing, Mama, Sing!"

THE ROOM WAS dark and damp as humidity encircled my head. My throat ached in pain as I tried to swallow. I gasped and strained to fill my lungs with air. Panic caused my heart to race. I was scared — I couldn't breathe. I was alone in the dark and afraid.

A deep, hoarse cough escaped from my small body and then in the darkness she came. A soft, gentle hand stroked my brow and patted my back as she lifted me to her warm lap. I strained the words, "sing, Mama, sing," and in the stillness of the night a tired voice sang those words of comfort, "God will take care of you …" As her sweet voice echoed in the darkness of the room, my heart quickly calmed. I breathed easier as I rested in the arms of my mother and her God.

As far back as I can remember, I knew there was something special about my mother and her relationship with God. My mother prayed about everything, and Jesus was mentioned every day around our house, but my earliest memory of prayer was when I had the croup. Having the croup was a very scary thing for me, not being able to breathe. But my mother's prayers for me and her voice singing "God will take care of you" or

"Safe is Thea, in the hallow of His hands" seemed to calm me like nothing else could. I can still remember the peacefulness I felt as she would rock me in her lap and sing.

I was born in 1949. Life at that time was hard for most people, and my parents were no different. With one son, age 17, and a daughter, age 10, the last thing they needed was another baby! But my mother was pregnant, and life was difficult to say the least! She was worried about how they would make it with another child on the way, when it already took all they had to survive. At almost 40 years of age, she panicked at the reality of another child. Her older sister told her that this child may be the "child of her travail" but would also be the "child of great promise" for her.

The child of travail surfaced quite early since I was, from the beginning, a very strong-willed child. As I entered my teen years, my strong will blossomed into rebellion against all authority: my parents, the school, the church and even the law. But through it all, my parents continued to love me, pray for me, discipline me and set a godly example for me. Eventually I married and left home. "Now," I thought, "I can do whatever I want!" But God had His hand on me and 2,000 miles away from home living in Denver, Colorado, I finally faced myself. It was an ugly sight. I knelt by my bed, all alone, and met with God. I confessed my sin, accepted the gift of the blood of Christ shed on the cross for my forgiveness, and received a new life "in Christ." God burst into my life that day and since that time I have never been the same.

I wish I could say that my life was a bowl of cherries after that, but it was not so. I had much to learn about living the life of surrender to God's will. I had been adopted into the family of God that day in Colorado, but just as a child needs nourishment to be healthy, so I needed daily food that would show me who God is, what He had done and how to walk by faith in His promises. A painful life was to be my tutor and the Bible my guide, leading me to the only place I could find rest, at the feet of Jesus.

I have often asked God why we have to go through so many hurts—why life has to be so hard and sometimes the pain so long. But now, as I review my life and welcome my senior citizen self, I realize that all life teaches us by experience what I learned in a cold, dark room in the arms of my mother.

My mother had Alzheimer's. My siblings and I watched our mother decline in health and wondered why the Lord kept her here for so long, slowly losing herself to the disease. She obviously loved the Lord and His Word and longed to be with Him in heaven, but He waited and we lost much of who she was to us.

She lived in an elderly care facility nearby, and I always visited her on the weekends. Sometimes she would smile and ask me, "How is your mother doing?" and I would tell her "She's just fine!" With a big smile she would say, "She's really such a nice lady!" I would laugh and agree that she was a nice lady, a sweet lady.

At times I think the Lord left her here for others to watch her sweet childlike manner. As we traveled through our own trials of faith, she was forever singing and smiling and thanking God for everything and for everybody. All the nurses would tell me, "Your mother is so sweet. It's like her childlike mind is stuck in 'glad mode.'" The Spirit of the One she loved for so long still glowed from her face in childlike trust.

Still the voice singing in the night to me: "God will take care of you ..."

"Oh, magnify the Lord with me and let us exalt His Name together! I will praise the Name of God with a song; I will magnify Him with thanksgiving. My soul magnifies the Lord, and my spirit rejoices in God, my Savior" (Psalm 34:3; 69:30).

3
A Tribute to My Mother

I VENTURE TO say that at least once in every girl's lifetime, she wants to be a princess!

Like little boys, who on rainy days tie bath towels around their necks and swoop down on villains and rescue beautiful women in distress, little girls dream of faraway places. They dream of golden castles hidden in thick forests and knights in shining armor and the high and lofty life of the beautiful princess who lives there! And of course, I am no different. Yes, I also dreamed of being a princess!

I remember my parents' closet—it was tiny and dark with a faint musty smell. There was one small light hanging from the ceiling on a long golden chain. Their closet told the story of their life. In the '40s and '50s, life was simple. My parents lived a very meager lifestyle. There were few clothes in their closet. All were worn. Their everyday work clothes were plain and durable with a few patches here and there. Then, they had their Sunday "go-to-meeting" clothes, which were few. My mother was a tiny woman with small, delicate feet. She had one pair of high-heeled shoes. They stood by themselves in the darkest corner of the closet against the wall: black open-toed patent leather high-heeled shoes.

I loved them!

Many times I would sneak away into the dark closet—my secret "forest"—and ascend into my beautiful make-believe castle in the sky. I would slip my chubby little feet into those black patent leather high heels and they became my magical shoes!

An air of royalty began to flow through my veins with my first step! I was a beautiful princess locked away in the golden castle, waiting for my handsome prince to come and rescue me and take me to the land of everlasting happiness. My handsome prince would slay dragons as I twirled around and around in my magical shoes, bobbing my head up and down under my parents' coattails. I could only stay in the magic for a few minutes before I would hear my mother call to me, "Thea, where are you? Come here right this minute!" I would wiggle my little toes out of her shoes and run to my mother's side. In my world of make-believe, my mother always brought me back to reality … and safety.

This Sunday is Mother's Day. I have been thinking about my mother often. What a wonderful mother she was, and I am forever grateful to her. Of course, there are many obvious reasons that I hold her with such endearment. She loved me unconditionally.

She loved me faithfully when I was very hard to love. I was her wild and rebellious child, wanting to live in a world of my own choosing, where I was not only the princess but also the queen and the king, always doing whatever I wanted!

My stubbornness and selfishness broke her heart. To love someone and see them go headstrong into destruction, not being able to stop them, is heart-rending. But for her love and forgiveness and unending prayer for me, I will be forever grateful. But that is not what I am most thankful for.

More than 30 years ago, my mother, in her declining years, stood in my doorway and again, with that look of love and anguish I knew so well, looked me straight in the eyes and said. "Thea, when will you ever listen? Your life will never change until you humble yourself and start your day on your knees, before the Lord, in prayer and in His Word. You talk too much … you need to learn to listen. Only His Word brings peace, and you must seek Him on your own."

And I did.

In desperation, I began my life journey to start my day early, on my knees, reading His Word, the Bible, over and over and over again.

"In the beginning was the Word and the Word was with God and the Word was God. All things came into being by Him and apart from Him nothing came into being that has come into being. In Him was Life and the Life was the Light of man. He was in the beginning with God. And the Word became flesh and dwelt among us and we beheld His glory, the glory as of the Only Begotten of the Father, full of grace and truth. Your Word is my comfort in my affliction. Your Word has given me hope. Your Word is a lamp unto my feet. Your Word is a light to my path. Your Word is sent forth and brings healing. I have hidden Your Word in my heart so I will not sin against You. Your Word is my delight. At your feet there are pleasures forevermore" (John 1:1-4, 14; Psalm 16:11; 107:20; 119:11, 24, 49-50, 105).

When I was a little girl, my mother taught me everything:

how to cook, clean, wash and iron, sew, sing, and pray and last-
ly, how to die. But what I remember most about my mother is
that she knew God—she didn't just know ABOUT God, she
KNEW God. She knew God through His Holy Word and her
Blessed Savior and Eternal Joy.

My mother was a simple woman. She was a woman of contentment. A happy woman. A woman of wisdom. A woman of
godliness.

You can imitate goodness with good deeds but godliness
can't be imitated. It is Christ-inside, shining out through a heart
humbled and devoted to the Master.

So on this, another Mother's Day, I thank you, Mother, for
your love and care and faithfulness. But I thank you mostly for
loving God the most!

*"Charm is deceitful, and beauty is passing, but a woman who fears the
Lord, she shall be praised" (Proverbs 31:30).*

4
Go Forth Weeping ...
Come Back Rejoicing

SITTING ALONE, HER left arm leaning on the wooden bench in front of her, she laid her head down and softly cried. Silently she poured her concerns out to the God she could not see.

Her problems, whispered from her lips, were strangling the life from her. Feeling she had nowhere to turn for help, she went there—a hot, empty church—to sit and pray.

My mother often told me the story about the day her life changed.

I was just a small child at the time. She was in her early 40s and immersed in problems: money issues, marital problems, drama of extended family. She wanted to live in peace but couldn't make it happen. Things were going from bad to worse, and she went there to be alone.

She had a key to the church, Warrington Presbyterian Church, where my parents were charter members and my father was a deacon at the time.

Exhausted from prayer and emptied from all her concerns, she kept repeating the name of Jesus, "Jesus, Jesus, Jesus ..."

She softly sang to her Savior, and then she felt it, a touch on her shoulder. Surprised, thinking she was alone, she quickly turned around only to see no one there. She turned in the other direction, but still no one. Then she heard it, a deep inner voice that said, "Jo, come away with me and rest."

She told me that she felt a wonderful peace come over her. As she sat there and pondered what had happened and what she heard, she knew it was the voice of God speaking to her weary heart.

That was the day my mother changed and she began her journey into the "trysting" place, as she would refer to her quiet time with the Lord.

If you are like me, you may not know what that word means: trysting. It's certainly not used much, so what is a trysting place? Webster's defines it as a secret rendezvous between two lovers.

God had done something to my mother. God is always the initiator of everything He does. The Bible tells us that we love Him because He first loved us. Only God can awaken our dull souls to desire seeking Him so that we can love Him with all our heart, mind and soul. Loving God requires a loving God. He was calling my mother deeper into the knowledge and love of God through His Word.

So what could that 40-something woman do? She followed. She tasted love from the well that never runs dry.

The next morning, she began a pattern she followed for the rest of her life.

She would wake up by 4 a.m. to seek God, to praise, to pray and to see Him as He would reveal Himself in His Holy Word, the Bible. Those words, "Jo, come away with me and rest," forever changed her life … and mine too, in time.

I am a preacher's wife. When I was a child, I never, ever, ever wished that to happen! I was my mother's wild child, so being married to a preacher would have been outrageous to me! But here I am, married, and I might add, very happily married, to a preacher!

If you spend a lot of time in church, you learn the term "prayer warrior."

That term refers to people who pray a lot and seem to have answers to their prayers. It refers to people who do battle, not WITH people but FOR people. They battle not with harsh words and anger but with faith and gentleness and wisdom. They do not flaunt their good deeds, but through tears shed alone they hold the promises of God up to God in faith. Prayer warriors find their rest with Him alone. Prayer warriors know they are nothing, but their God is everything. They know that He is in control, and His grace is always sufficient. Prayer warriors know they are just a broken vessel that the Lord is using to accomplish His plan. They pray continually, not to change God because they know He never changes and always knows best. But through their prayers, they carry others and lay them at His feet, trusting only in his Word and in His will.

"Those who go forth weeping, carrying seed to sow, will return with songs of joy, carrying sheaves with them" (Psalm 126:6).

My mother's life changed that day in that hot, empty church, and over time she became a prayer warrior. I know that firsthand! She did battle FOR me, along with many others. She took us to the only One who could open blind eyes and give life to dead hearts. She rested there with Him, just like He told her she would, so many, many years ago.

I don't think my mother ever prayed for me to marry a preacher, but she did pray for me to know the Lord and to love Him with all my heart, mind and soul. In God's kindness and His providence, He gave me to a preacher. I believe one of the highest callings a woman can have is to love and pray for the one whom God has called to hold His Word out to others. My marriage has been one of God's greatest blessings of grace for this little "wild" thing! Now, I too "go forth weeping, carrying seed to sow," and I know I "will return with songs of joy, carrying sheaves with me!"

Thank you, Lord! Thank you, mother! Thank you, husband!

"Grow in the grace and knowledge of our Lord and Savior Jesus Christ. To Him be the glory both now and forever" (2 Peter 3:18).

5
Morning Sounds

SNUGGLED IN A little ball, resting between fresh-smelling sheets that just the day before had danced in the sunlight on my mother's clothesline, my ears opened to the sounds of the morning.

In the distant woods behind our house, I could hear the wake-up call of many different birds that graced our woods. The mockingbird was my favorite. He was the first to sing each morning. His voice was a restful lullaby that would almost lull me back to sleep. But then I would hear the blue jay, brash and loud, announcing his entrance into the day. My mother always told me that the blue jay was "too big for his britches." He was always the first to eat the food she left out each morning and seemed to love stealing it from the smaller, more timid birds. Within minutes, our woods were filled with a symphony of sounds. I kept my eyes tightly closed and listened, pulling the sheets over my head. I snuggled into my warm little nest. I loved it here!

The aroma of frying bacon and freshly brewed coffee filled the air, signaling the day was soon to begin for me, and I must rise from my warm little bed and greet the day.

I think one of the first memories of my mornings as a

child was the sound of birds and my mother whistling. My mother loved to whistle, and she was quite good at it! She almost sounded like the little birds in the woods. I recognized the tunes. They were the ones we sang at church: "Love Lifted Me," "Blessed Assurance," and "Heavenly Sunshine." Her music filled our kitchen, mixing with the sounds of her frying bacon and washing dishes.

Even though my day was just beginning, I knew my mother's day had begun hours before. My mother had her "date" with God every morning around 4 o'clock. I knew she read her Bible, a lot. It was all marked up, and some of the pages were worn thin. I knew she prayed for all of us because I peeked in her books and saw our names written all over the pages. And my mother was always singing! I loved her voice. There was peacefulness in it and at the same time exploding joy! Her old hymnal looked like her Bible—all underlined in red with names written everywhere.

As I grew up I wondered how anyone could possibly pray for such a long time. It seemed to me, in my little girl mind, that you would just run out of stuff to say! I would ask my mother about this and she would smile and say, "The time flies by when you're with the One you love."

It was many years later that I realized my mother was not just talking to God for three hours every morning. She was listening. Just like me, snuggled up in my little bed listening to the melody of the birds, she snuggled in the arms of her Lord and listened to Him in His Holy Word.

I had to learn for myself that life is so full of the talking and the doing, and yet it is in the listening that we learn the secret of true happiness. My mother learned to listen to what God said in His Word, to surrender and trust in His goodness and mercy and accept each day as a gift from Him, whatever that day might bring.

I guess that's why she whistled as she went about her daily chores. She had been "found by God" and she could see His hand on every part of her life, not only in the quiet times of meditation, but also in the busyness of a woman's life—cooking meals, washing dishes, mopping floors and taking care of a strong-willed, chubby little tan girl!

She had been to the fountain of living water long before the dawn. She drank deeply, and His joy and peace bubbled out, and she just had to whistle!

I wish I could be that little girl again, just one more time, to wake up to the feel and smell of those sheets and to lie still in my little bed, listening to the birds in the woods and to hear my mother whistling in the kitchen.

"Still other seed fell on good soil. It came up and yielded a crop, a hundred times more than was sown. When He said this, He called out, whoever has ears to hear, let them hear" (Luke 8:8).

"Thus said the Lord; Let not the wise man glory in his wisdom, let not the mighty man glory in is might, nor let the rich man glory in his riches; but let him that glories, glory in this, that he understands and knows Me, that I Am the Lord, exercising lovingkindness, judgement, and righteousness in the earth, for in these I delight, says the Lord" (Jeremiah 9:23-24).

6
Dusty Daydreams and Attic Treasures

"I will go before you and make the crooked places straight; I will break in pieces the gates of bronze and cut the bars of iron. I will give you the treasures of darkness and hidden riches of secret places that you may know that I, The Lord, who call you by your name, Am the God of Israel" (Isaiah 45:2-3).

WHERE I UP grew up in the Deep South, September is still hot as "H-E-double-two-sticks," as my mother used to jokingly say!

October is the first real feel of cooler days!

I grew up without air conditioning. It's hard for me to even fathom that now, but that's just the way it was back then. Florida is hot, and it gets hotter and more humid each month of the summer, rising to its pinnacle in September! For children already back in school, also not air conditioned, September days were slow and salty. Perspiration dripping down your face, counting the hours until the bell would ring and you could ride your bicycle home, cooling in the afternoon breeze—the days were long! September summer would finally draw itself to a close and that heavenly month, October, would burst into bloom, ushering in cool mornings and crisp evenings and sometimes even cool days out on the red clay playground at recess. Fall weather in the south was finally here!

I remember early October mornings, waking up with a cool breeze brushing against my cheek. On Saturday mornings my mother let me sleep in. She would prop open the screen door in my bedroom that led to the backyard. She said she was letting the cool air and sunshine in! I think Saturday mornings in October are some of my fondest memories of my childhood. I would just lay there lingering in bed, feeling the coolness, listening to the sounds of the morning, smelling the delicious aroma from my mother's kitchen and just daydream.

And what a daydreamer I was! I envisioned how great my world would be when I grew up! When I wasn't just the "baby" in the family, when I didn't always have to do what my parents told me to do. I could go where I wanted and do what I wanted and, of course, I would have all the perfect people in my life and all the money I ever needed to do all those wonderful things I wanted to do … it would just have to wait until I grew up! Until then, I daydreamed!

I don't remember when the daydreaming turned into active rebellion, but its seeds surfaced quite early. While reading one of my mother's journals written when I was only 3 or 4 years old, one of her private prayers was about her "little angel Thea" who had such a rebellious streak! If only she had known when she wrote those words about the pain in her heart that her little angel would cause her one day. I'm glad she did not know what was ahead.

Rebellious seeds turned into prideful daydreaming, then into selfishness, and then into a full-blown life of rebellion!

And then, there was always Grace.

My mother had Alzheimer's. When we placed her in an elder-care facility, my siblings and I had to go through our old homestead and sort through a lifetime. Anyone who has had that task knows the happiness and the sadness it brings as you touch and sometimes discard the pieces of a life of one who loved you and cared for you. The parent becomes the child, and the child becomes the parent. It's very difficult and it pierces the heart with pain on many levels.

There are places of joy found in the sadness as you relive happy memories and forgotten events. You find saved birthday cards, a child's scribbled note stuffed into a Bible, or pictures you drew as a child. These are precious finds. But for me, discovering a large box in the attic containing my mother's prayer journals that she kept when I was a child became for me an oasis of hope, love and wisdom! To look into the private writings and prayers of the one who probably loved me more than any person on earth was a treasure beyond measure.

My mother referred to her quiet time with God as her "trysting" place. Not knowing what that word meant forced me to Webster's dictionary: trysting, a secret rendezvous of two lovers. Holding those little journals in my hand, I brushed the dust off and slowly began leafing through the thin yellowing pages; I peered into the divine romance of a quiet little woman and her Mighty God. I began seeing into the center of who she was and why. For years I had walked in the circle of her love and grace but now, as she was declining in health, I was given the privilege of seeing into the real woman she was. Reading her beautiful ink script, I saw her helplessness, her honesty, her neediness and gazed upon the God of the Bible that was her only hope, her only security, her only JOY. Her strength was manifested in her weakness as she depended on the God she knew from being in His Word for so many, many years.

This was taken from my mother's journal, dated May 6, 1953 (I was 4 years old):

"Thank you Father for Thy healing hands upon Thea's croup; she was happier today. May my love for her, this day, guide and direct her gently but firmly and may she feel Thee in me. Father, rule out of ME impatience, injustice and irritation. Fill me with Thy Holy Spirit so it is THEE that works out all the problems. Let me be an example before her—purge and rebuke me and whip me into line, Father—no matter the cost, so that I will never be a stumbling block to any of my children. Cleanse me that I may be a fit vessel to lay my little Thea upon Thy altar. In reality I know she is all yours. Help me to relinquish her entirely to Thee to do with her what Thou wilt and in praise and thanksgiving, let me rest. I will lift up mine eyes to the hills from whence cometh my help. My help is from the Lord who made the heavens and the earth. In Thee do I put my trust."

Long before my rebellion bloomed and reared its ugly head, there was Grace, a little mother praying for me. Taking me to the only place there is refuge, to the altar of the Sovereign God! Did I know that? Of course not, I was only a "fidgety little 4-year-old! But my parents loved me and saw the truth about me and knew that I needed what they could never give me ... a Savior that would make the crooked places straight. She knew the God that created me and she prayed He would call me by name one day. And so year after year she went to the altar of God, holding up His Word to Him for her children.

Peeking into the intimacy she shared with the Lord through her writings exposed my shallow praying for my own children. I recalled how, throughout the years, my prayers for them had been mostly suggestions of what I thought they needed and pleading for Him to do this or that for them on short notice. I was ashamed of my shallowness. In my mother's journals, I saw a woman who pleaded for her Lord to search HER heart and convict HER and discipline HER and change HER into the image of Jesus so others might see HIM in her. Others (me included) she just laid at His feet, trusting that He knew what was best for His creations. Her eyes were fixed on Jesus, the author and finisher of her faith. Her desire was for His glory, whatever that entailed.

Those old dusty journals lying dormant for years in a dark attic became secret treasures to me. I prayed, "Thank You Lord, for a mother who took me to the throne of grace each morning to find mercy and help in her time of need. Thank you Lord, for calling me, for changing my rebellion into joy as I also live and rest in your Word and not in mine. I now dream of the day I will see You face to face and my faith will forever be lost to sight. Christ in me, my only hope of glory."

"That is, the mystery which has been hidden from the past ages and generations; but now has been manifested to His saints, to whom God willed to make known what is the riches of the glory of this mystery among the Gentiles, which is 'Christ in you, the hope of glory.' And

we proclaim HIM, admonishing every man and teaching every man with all wisdom, that we may present every man complete in Christ. And for this purpose also I labor, striving according to His power, which mightily works within me" (Colossians 1:26-29).

1
The Big Word

"THEA JUDITH …"

My mother always used my middle name when she wanted me to pay attention and listen to her!

"Wash your hands, eat all your vegetables, don't interrupt, say please, say thank you, and mind your manners!"

My little ears heard those words of instructions from my mother many, many times. She said that if I didn't listen then I would have to "feel." Sometimes I heard those words and quickly obeyed but when I didn't, she gave me a little helping hand that I would receive on my "fanny," as she called it.

But now the chubby little tan girl has THOSE instructions down pat! I know for certain what they mean and usually, I obey them.

But for the most part, I lived in my own little pretend world. I didn't go to school yet and most of my time was lived outside in our yard or on the beach with my mother and her best friend, Ms. Thelma, or in the woods behind our house playing with friends. In MY world, I was always the center of attention! In MY world, I was the princess or the teacher or the mama, but whoever I was, I was definitely in charge! I only listened to others when it was absolutely necessary!

The chubby little tan girl also learned another very important thing: how to tune out her parents' voices. Parents had grown-up talk, and I tuned it out instinctively. I didn't need to listen to it and I wasn't the least bit interested in their big-people world!

But at times, I did hear some very big words that I kind of wondered what they meant.

One of those big words I heard from my mother was "te-stapatience."

It was a big, long word, and I did not have a clue as to what it meant.

I played, I pretended and I kept hearing that word.

After a while I realized I was hearing it a lot!

One day while playing in my little world of make-believe, not listening to my mother at all, she called me a NAME! The only names my mother ever called me were sweet names, like precious and sweetie or her little angel, but this time, my mother CALLED me the BIG word, testapatience!

She said I was her testapatience!

I was still clueless, although it must not have been good because her face looked very different than her "precious little Thea" face.

I laugh today as I think of that.

This morning during my quiet time with the Lord, I hear our youngest 7-month-old grandson begin to school his parents in this long and powerful word, testapatience!

They are visiting from Michigan for the Thanksgiving holidays, and each morning, very early, I hear his sweet little voice.

He's awake before 5 a.m., and his parents are very sleepy!

"Precious" is wide awake, playing and singing and then eventually … fussing. There is no stopping it. He wins and "school is in session."

Someone has to get up, fix a bottle, fight back the tired and sleepy eyes and take care of the kid!

Since mommy had her session at midnight, daddy has been enrolled for the early-morning session.

Children are a blessing from the Lord and will fill our hearts with some of the greatest pleasures we will ever experience. But yes, they are certainly the BIG word, a testapatience!

In the book of James, we are given instructions to "count it all joy when you fall into various trials, knowing that the testing of your faith produces patience. But let it have its perfecting work, that you may be mature and complete, lacking nothing."

Deuteronomy 8:2-3 says, "You shall remember that the Lord your God led you all the way these 40 years in the wilderness to humble you and test you, to know what was in your heart, whether you would keep his commandments or not. So He humbled you, allowing you to hunger, fed you with manna which you did not know nor did your fathers know, that He might make you know, that man shall not live by bread alone but by every Word that proceeds from the mouth of the Lord."

Trials and tests are given to us to humble us and to show us what's in our heart, which is usually NOT a pretty picture! We are to be patient, but we are impatient and irritated instead. We may have learned to muzzle our outward complaining but God sees the heart and He knows we don't have what it takes and so we gripe, complain and blame others!

And then in exasperation and impatience we call out to God

to help us! And He does!

Trials and tests give us a taste of our own shallowness as we try to drink deeply from our own empty cup!

In our wilderness we become hungry and thirsty for something other than our own way of solving life's problems!

We pray and think, "Perhaps God has a Word for me" … weary from the test, I strain to hear.

"Come to me, all who are weary and I will give you rest" (Matthew 11:28).

As the chubby little tan girl wore out my mother's patience, she fled to the only source of patience—God himself. He humbled the little mother as she faced her own lack, and He taught her by experience that "man shall not live by bread alone but by every Word that proceeded from the mouth of God" (Matthew 4:4).

I was NOT my parents' easy child by any means! I have my mother's old journals, written during my childhood, that are filled with prayers for her precious little angel, Thea, her strong-willed child!

But I WAS God's tool in my mother's life to help her grow and mature, to stretch her faith, to humble her and cause her to pray. Where else could she go but to God to get help raising this strong-willed little girl!

When she was bone-tired, I did not care—I was just a kid. She put my needs first anyway.

When I was a teenager and thought I hated her, she loved me and prayed for me anyway.

Yes, I was her testapatience and God changed her … she became a prayer warrior, a lover of the Bible and the most patient, humble and godly woman I have ever known!

I miss you, mama, and thank you so much for loving the tool of God's testapatience in your life. I have learned so much from your example and others are still learning as I pass on in my little stories what you taught me in your unassuming ways in a little cottage in Beach Haven so many, many years ago.

So what's your trial today, or should I ask, "Who is your testapatience"?

Your testapatience may possibly be the greatest blessing you will ever know, especially if it puts you on your knees, in God's Word, seeking the source of patience: God Himself!

Anything that causes you to pray is indeed a blessing!

"Count it all joy my brothers when you meet trials of various kinds, for you know that the testing of your faith produces patience. And let patience have its full effect, so that you may be mature and complete lacking nothing. If any of you lacks wisdom; let him ask God who gives generously to all without reproach and it will be given him, but let him ask in faith with no doubting, for the one who doubts is like a wave of the sea that is driven and tossed by the wind. For that person must not suppose that he will receive anything from the Lord; he is double minded man, unstable in all his ways" (James 1:2-8).

8
"Line Up!"

"LINE UP, CLASS!" Those words echoed through our classroom.

I wasn't sure what she meant ... line up?

It was my first day of school.

A chubby little girl, tan from playing in the sun most of the summer, hearing those words—"be still," "don't talk," and now, "line up." Those words were foreign to my mind.

My life had been one of adventure!

My days were spent building tree forts and teepees in the woods behind our house or spending hours and hours designing elaborate sandcastles on the beach or bread jugging for minnows down on the bayou where I lived. My life was full of make-believe and magnificent dreams.

And now, here I am in this "school place" that my parents said I needed, listening to commands I did not understand—it was strange indeed.

My first-grade schoolteacher was Miss Bessie Ballard. It was my first week of first grade at Navy Point Elementary School. It was a new school and everything was nice and clean. My teacher went to our church, so I already knew her. My mother said she was a spinster. Later I came to know that meant she had never been married and now spent her life teaching other people's children. I was one of those.

Miss Ballard had always been nice to me at church. She and my mother were friends. She was kind of old, a little chubby like me, but she had a really sweet smile. She always seemed relaxed, like you just wanted to get up on her lap and let her hold you. I liked her and felt safe in her room, even though I did not know any of the other kids in my class.

After getting settled in my little wooden chair and desk and listening to Miss Ballard talk for a while, I heard this strange command: "Line up, class!"

I soon learned that "line up" meant we were going somewhere. It could be the playground or the bathroom or the lunchroom, but it was a destination that only Miss Ballard knew. Our job was just to quietly get up from our seats, stand one by one behind her, and then follow her to her desired destination. She was the leader; we were the followers.

As first-graders, Miss Ballard had to teach us the duties of the lineup!

First, we had to leave our position and move toward her. We had to learn to wait. We moved only when she moved. We did not go off on our own way, even if we knew a shortcut. There was no talking, just listening. Eyes were to be straight ahead on her, hands to ourselves, minding our own business.

This was really hard for the chubby little tan girl.

Miss Ballard said we were learning how to pay attention and control ourselves. It wasn't fun to be in line, but I soon realized it was the necessary mode of travel for all the little kids in the strange new place called school. I always liked it when we arrived at the destination, but the line thing was really a hassle for the chubby little tan girl.

After this group of unruly first-graders learned the basics of the lineup, Miss Ballard began choosing one of the especially talented rookies to be a line leader. Wow! This was the ultimate reward, the coveted prize for each little first grader: line leader!

But something strange seemed to happen to the line leader after they had been picked to lead once or twice: they seemed to morph into an ugly dictator. Somehow they started thinking they were better (a cut above the rest) than all the other rookie first-graders who had never made it to the front of the line. But like all dictators, their pride would ultimately cause a fall and they would be demoted to the back of the line. How great the fall. The humiliation of it all!

Jesus tells us if you want to be first, then take the place at the back of the line. It's the place where the humble live. First-graders and even grown-ups don't readily take the last place at the end of the line until humiliation first knocks at our door.

It knocked for me in first grade as a line leader.

Oh how I loved being chosen to be in front of everyone else! Strutting my first-grade "stuff" up to the front of the line, I held my head high. I believed that I was the greatest of all those little first-graders … Miss Ballard picked me to lead the line!

But, like most first-graders, it wasn't long before my fall. Not paying attention, minding other people's business, not keeping my hands to myself, talking too much. Doomed to fall!

Then it came. Miss Ballard called my name OUT LOUD in the lunchroom … in front of everyone!

"Thea, go back to the end of the line!" Horrified, I froze,

dropped my head with my lower lip quivering and began my descent from glory into shame.

It's a LONG walk to the back of the line. Eyes all staring at you. Laughing at you even though they don't say a word. It's too much to bear. You don't look at them, but you know the look because you've looked at others that same way.

Shuffling to the back, you take your place and sulk a while. But you are ignored in your pain.

Day after day, destination after destination, you travel at the back of the line. You actually begin to like it back there. You don't have to strut anymore because everyone has seen your fall. You don't impress anyone anymore. All you have to do is obey Miss Ballard.

Finally, you find that you are just content to be at the back of the line. Following Miss Ballard with your mouth closed, hands to your side, putting one foot in front of the other, not knowing where you are going but knowing Miss Ballard will get you there and you will like it.

Then one sun-shiny day out on the playground, tired from jumping rope, Miss Ballard catches my eye. "Thea, why don't you be line leader back to our classroom?"

Horrors upon horrors! My little first-grade mind whirling, "Oh no, not me. I don't want to be the line leader! I might mess up again and everyone will know—they will know I'm not great after all. I'm just a chubby little tan girl who often messes up. It's safer back here at the back of the line."

But she gave me a hug and smiled her sweet smile and said to me, "It's OK, Thea, you can do it."

And so I slowly walked up to the front of the line, quiet,

obedient, and followed Miss Ballard back to our classroom. I sat down in my little wooden chair at my desk and folded my hands. She smiled at me. I breathed easier. It felt nice.

Philippians 3:12 tells us, "Not that I have already obtained this or am already perfect, but I press on to make it my own, because Christ Jesus has made me his own." He says that I should "press on toward the goal for the prize of the upward call of God in Christ Jesus" (Philippians 3:14).

This "pressing on" in the life of faith we are living now has the root word meaning of "to LINE UP"! Imagine that! It comes from a military word that means to walk in a straight line, to keep in step, in rank, to be obedient and stay in the correct lane so you have a forward progressive movement. This kind of daily movement involves the disciplined and goal-orientated life to get you where you are meant to be.

The Lord Jesus is our line leader. Get up and follow Him. Listen to His voice, which you will hear in the Bible. Learn to be still, wait until He moves, keep your eyes ahead and your hands out of other people's business. Don't talk too much but learn to listen, pay attention, enjoy the walk and expect to get to His desired destination for you. Don't think too much about yourself, be content to stay at the back of the line or even at the front if He decides you need to be there for a while … just keep looking ahead at the Glory of God in the face of Jesus Christ!

"Everyone who exalts himself will be humbled and he who humbles himself will be exalted" (Luke 18:14).

"The lofty looks of man shall be humbled, the haughtiness of men shall be bowed down and the Lord alone shall be exalted" (Isaiah 2:11).

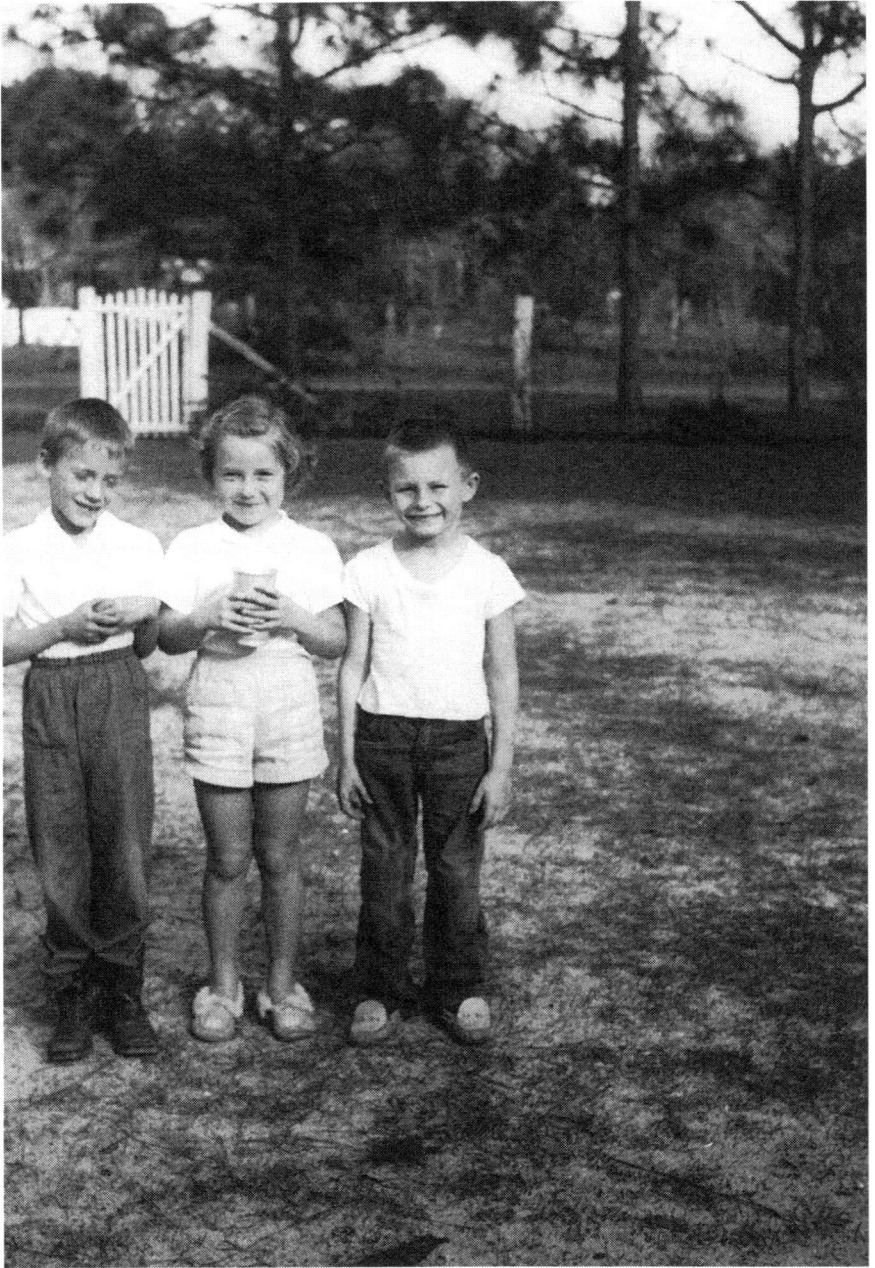

9
First-Grade Love

"OH, MAMA, I'M so excited! Only one more day and it will be Saturday!" I told my mother.

Saturday was a very special day for this little 7-year-old girl. Saturday was grocery shopping day and that meant a trip in the car up to Warrington, a little suburb of Pensacola, Florida.

But this shopping day was extra special because I would be able to do some shopping of my own! That didn't happen often, as our family was like most families in the early '50s: a stay-at-home mom and a father who worked really hard just to make ends meet, living from paycheck to paycheck with little to spare. We would probably be classified as a low-income family but without any government assistance. My parents worked hard and made it on their own.

I didn't realize at the time that we didn't have much, for I had everything I needed: parents who loved me, a warm bed to sleep in, good food every day, wide open spaces to play in and build forts. I would often pretend I was an Indian princess who lived in the make-believe teepees I had constructed with palmetto leaves and pine straw. Life was grand in my little world!

But this Saturday was an extra special shopping day for me.

It would soon be Valentine's Day, and my mother said I could pick out my own valentine cards!

All week long at school my class had been preparing for our valentine party. Big brown grocery bags were delicately trimmed with red and pink construction paper hearts and little doilies with "I love you" written on them. It was gloriously fun, but all the while everyone was wondering just who would drop a valentine into their bags. The suspense was exhilarating, and we could hardly wait for the big day to come for our classroom party.

But now, I had to attend to the business of picking out my valentine cards. I took the job seriously—the ones I picked out had to be very special. I jumped into our big old green Oldsmobile and within minutes my mother was at the grocery store. I could hardly wait to get to the valentine card aisle.

Oh, there were just so many to pick from—how could I just pick one package? But I knew there was only money enough for one so I had to be very sure they were just right! Did I want the silly ones with Betty Boop or the pretty ones with flowers and hearts and mushy words all over them? I paced up and down the aisle and finally picked out the ones I liked best. I carefully handed them to my mother, who placed them in the steel grocery cart along with our groceries. While my mother finished shopping, my mind was whirling. The really big job lay before me: What person would get what card? Just the very thought of it made my heart race!

Later that night I carefully looked at each card and finally made my decision. I neatly printed names on each card, licked the envelope and went to bed with little red hearts and cupids dancing in my dreams.

Monday morning came and my mother tied a ribbon around my little package of valentines. She gave me a kiss on the forehead and a tiny pink candy heart that said "I love you" and sent me off to school.

All the children in class anxiously awaited the party scheduled for later that day. You could hear whispers from the little boys and giggles from the girls as they talked about who would be their valentine. The day seemed to drag on for hours on end, but finally the teacher told us to put away our pencils and paper and get out our valentines. Oh, my heart was really pounding now! The room was lined with beautifully decorated brown paper bags all taped to the wall. Finally, with a nod from the teacher, we began the silent and solemn job of dropping our valentines into the bags. After the last child sat down, the teacher carefully presented each bag and the treasures it held to each child. I took my bag and peeked inside. It was filled to the brim with envelopes, big ones, little ones and ones with little heart candies on top.

I carefully opened each valentine and read the printed name on the back. I counted them all, once, twice and then again. A big smile spread all over my chubby little face. I had so many friends. I liked everyone, and everyone liked me. There was one from every friend in my class. And yes, even a real mushy one with flowers on it that said "I love you" with X's and O's from the little neighbor boy I thought was so cute. He smiled at me when I opened his card. I giggled.

Just then, the bell rang and it was time to go. Picking up paper scraps and wiping icing off my desk, I gathered up my valentines and lined up to go home.

How times flies! I'm now grown up but the memories of simple days live on and the excitement still makes me smile.

First-grade love is sweet and simple. Big-people love … not so easy.

What does real love actually look like?

I look at my own heart at times and think I am still writing valentine cards wanting the Betty Boop version of first-grade love.

So where do I look to see it?

I can look back at my parents and see love. They did love each other and were married almost 50 years before my father passed away. But still their love was not perfect by any means. My mother told me stories of their "love life." She fell in love with my father when she was only 14 years old. She was 17 when they ran away to get married. Life was not the way she envisioned it would be at all! She told me she cried a lot. One night she got up in the middle of the night and walked to her mother's house, thinking she would just move back in with her parents. Her mother told her she did not live there anymore: "Go back where you belong." A harsh lesson to learn but it forced her to make a commitment to the man she was married to, for better or worse, as she had promised God. Love did not feel so good then, but she stayed and she prayed.

My mother told me that eventually they changed—left the elementary stages of love—as they both learned to yield to the Lord. He taught them how to love each other. He loved through them. Because I was the baby in the family, I saw the grown-up version of their love.

It looked like this:

"Love is patient and kind; love does not envy or boast; it is not arrogant or rude. It does not insist on its own way; it is not irritable or resentful; it does not rejoice at wrongdoing, but rejoices with the truth. Love bears all things, believes all things, hopes all things, endures all things. Love never ends" (1 Corinthians 13:4-8).

Grown-up love gives ...

"For God so loved the world that He gave His only begotten Son that whosoever believes in Him shall not perish but have everlasting life" (John 3:16).

"A new commandment I give to you that you love one another, as I have loved you, you also love one another. By this, all will know you are My disciples, if you have love for one another" (John 13:34-35).

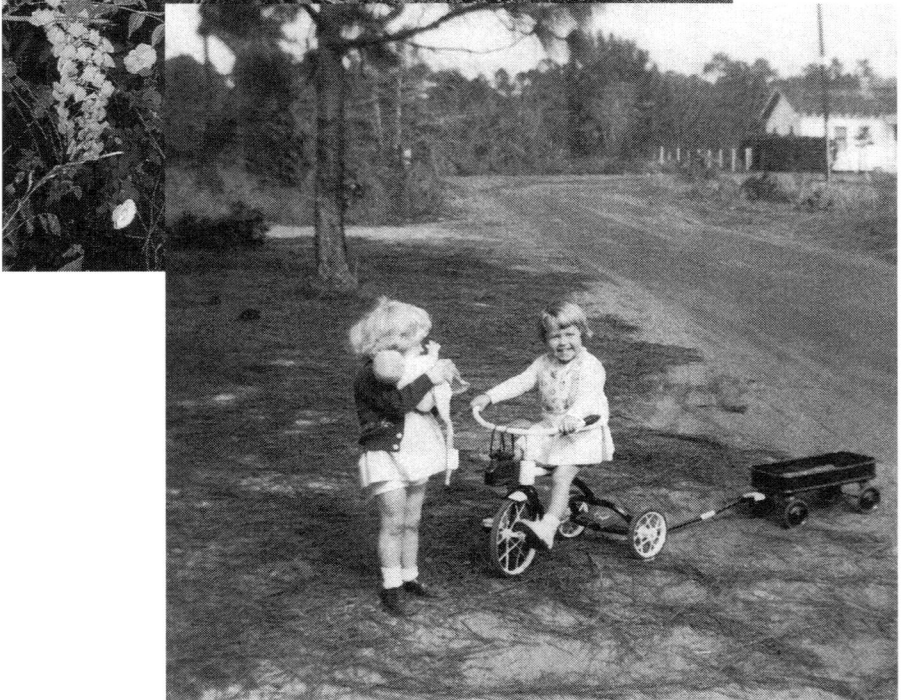

10
Flower Bush Forts

THERE IS SOMETHING heavenly about lying in wisteria blossoms—purple and white petals as a soft fragrant bedspread! And so I remember of my secret hideaway in my "flower bush forts."

Both my parents loved flowers. We had lots of them in our yard. My father built our house during the depression. It was not a fancy house, but strong, sound and sturdy, like my father. It was a little white cottage, built in the woods, near the beach, and the lot was full of scrub oaks, palmetto bushes and sandy soil.

My mother loved the delicate, beautiful things. Little by little, year after year, she toiled in the yard. She was always pulling up weeds, sprigging grass, fertilizing, mulching and tending with love that sandy soil. And she loved planting flowers … lots of flowers! Some of them grew year after year, multiplying over time, but some were seasonal and changed each year as the mood of springtime would catch her fancy!

Amid the array of colors and blossoms, there were several that seemed to dominate our yard. They were the azalea, Camilla, gardenia and the wisteria vine. My mother had grown quite an array of these during the years they lived in their Beach Haven cottage. As springtime came, there was an explosion of colors and fragrance, and I loved it! That was my time to build my secret flower bush forts.

It was painstaking work. I would grab my little red wagon and patrol the yard, looking for an opening in an azalea bush that was large enough for me to squeeze in and build my "fort"! Once I spied the perfect bush, I began collecting flowers to line the floor of my secret fort. I would drag my little red wagon along the borders of our yard, searching for beautiful blossoms that had fallen to the ground.

My last task was to reach up as high as my little arms could reach and pull down the wisteria vines that draped around the tall pines in our yard. The vines would drop to the ground around my feet. I began slowly pulling the purple petals off the vines and layering them on top of the other flowers in my little red wagon. Loaded down with all my treasures, I squeezed my chubby little body into my azalea fort and began covering the dirt floor with the precious petals.

After the floor was completely covered, I would lie down gently, be still and look up. No one knew I was there. It was my secret place. I could see the blue skies high above the azalea branches and hear the birds in the distant woods.

But the greatest pleasure was the fragrance. It was all around me: over me, under me. I can still remember that feeling and the sweet aroma in my flower bush fort.

God's love now fills me like that. I go into my secret place with Him in prayer. Hidden in Christ, away from the world, a child, not knowing all the answers but resting in the arms of my Heavenly Father, trusting and enjoying the sweet aroma of His tender touch, the fragrance of His love and the joy of His presence.

"You are my hiding place; you will protect me from trouble and surround me with songs of deliverance" (Psalm 32:7).

"If then you were raised with Christ, seek those things which are above where Christ is sitting at the right hand of God. Set your mind on things above, not on things on the earth. For you died and your life is hidden with Christ in God. When Christ who is your life appears, then you also will appear with Him in glory" (Colossians 3:1-4).

"And when you pray, you shall not be like the hypocrites. For they love to pray standing up in the synagogues and on the corners of the streets, that they may be seen by men. Assuredly, I say to you that they have their reward. But you, when you pray, go into your room and when you have shut your door, pray to your Father who is in the secret place; and your Father who sees in secret will reward you openly. And when you pray do not use vain repetitions as the heathen do. For they think that they will be heard for their many words. Therefore, do not be like them. For your Father knows the things you have need of before you ask Him. In this manner, therefore, pray:

Our Father in heaven, hallowed be Your name, Your kingdom come, Your will be done, on earth as it is in heaven. Give us this day our daily bread and forgive us our debts as we forgive us our debtors. And do not lead us into temptation but deliver us from the evil one. For Yours is the kingdom and the power and the glory forever. Amen" (Matthew 6:5-13).

11

Glory Gazing

HOT AND SWEATY little kids were pushing their way to the front of the line. Hands waving in the air trying to get her attention, voices shouting, "Pick me, JoJo, pick me!"

"JoJo" was what everyone affectionately called my mother.

Our neighborhood was like one big family. Most of us had lived on that dirt street in the middle of the woods our entire lives, which at that time for me was about 8 or 9 years. My parents built our house in the early '40s, and we were very close to all our neighbors.

Most of the dads worked at the naval air station, and the moms stayed home. None of us had much money but always enough of what was needed. We did not have air conditioning or TV, so we played outside! We pretended, and we had FUN!

Every once in a while, we would have a "spat," as JoJo called it, but it was never a big deal. All the moms in the neighborhood treated us the same, like their own kids. The rules were essentially the same. "Be nice, share, don't fight, mind your manners or I'll send you home and tell your daddy what you did." We sure did not want THAT to happen, so we learned to forgive, apologize, mind our manners and just go outside and play again. Life was good!

But we all looked forward to that special day when we could be better than everyone else! We could be made "much of" by all our buddies. That day was our birthday!

Because my birthday fell late in summer before school started, I always celebrated my birthday with my neighborhood friends.

Today is my big day, August the 9th! JoJo always made sure the chubby little tan girl had a birthday celebration! Ice cream, red sugary Kool-Aid, cupcakes with creamy chocolate icing with little colorful sprinkles! And we played games! Blind-folding each other with one of my mother's church scarves, we played pin the tail on the donkey, then on to red light/green light, but by far my favorite was the clothespin in the bottle game! That game took real skill to be able to drop my mother's clothespins into the small mouth of an empty glass milk bottle positioned at your feet. I became really good at it and hoped I'd win! Of course, I had been practicing before my party!

I love thinking about those times long ago and appreciate a mother who made sure her chubby little tan girl felt special, even though there was very little money to spend on presents.

But there was one very special present.

I don't remember exactly how old I was when I first looked at the "something" that changed my life. But I was small, like the gift: a colorful cardboard tube I could hold in my hand. No batteries needed.

What was it?

JoJo said, "Hold it up to your eye, Thea, and look up to the sky."

I couldn't believe what I saw. My little 8-year-old eye saw

an explosion of colors! Mama said, "Twist it just a little and keep looking up."

I just stood there immobilized in our front yard, looking up, holding the little cardboard tube to my eye.

She leaned down and whispered in my ear, "It's beautiful, isn't it?"

A big smile spread across my chubby round face, grateful for my present ... the little cardboard tube of majestic beauty! Every turn a new combination of colors and shapes! I was totally fascinated with the little tube of unending "glory gazing" in my kaleidoscope!

This morning in my quiet time with the Lord, I read Psalm 149:5: "Let the saints be JOYFUL in glory! Let them sing aloud on their beds!"

I remember that feeling of a little 8-year-old, being joyful in the glory of sunshine and beautiful colors and shapes that came out of the little cardboard tube that I held to my eye and looked up to the sky!

The word kaleidoscope actually means beautiful form watcher!

I am so grateful for my little mother who taught me to watch for the beauty of God's glory!

There is so much of His glory everywhere we look when we just stop long enough to gaze.

Take a minute and look at the wildflowers and the little bees gathering pollen, relish in the laughter from your child's face. Smile and enjoy the feel of holding the hand of the one you love. Stop, look up and watch the changing colors of the sky at daybreak, or if you're not a morning person, take time to seek a sunset! Watch it and be grateful. Actually "feel your smallness" and be overwhelmed by the glory of GOD! He's watching, and He takes pleasure in us noticing His handiwork!

Don't waste the moment ... Oh, it's gone now!

"Both young men and maidens; old men and children. Let them praise the Name of the Lord, for His name ALONE is exalted, His glory above the earth and heaven. Praise the Lord! Sing to the Lord a new song, and His praise in the assembly of the saints. Let Israel rejoice in their Maker; let the children of Zion be joyful in their King; Let the saints be JOYFUL IN GLORY; let them sing aloud on their beds" (Psalm 149:1-3, 5).

"Let everything that has breath praise the Lord. Praise the Lord!" (Psalm 150:6).

12
The Pine Straw Queen

MY CHUBBY LITTLE hands fumbled around and I finally grabbed the sides of the wheelbarrow to balance myself. I could feel the prickly stings of the pointed pine straw needles on the back of my legs. The air was crisp, and I felt my chubby cheeks flushed from the cool breeze on that November morning.

It was Saturday. My father was off from his regular job at the naval air station. My father worked all the time. He rose early during the week for his civil service job with the Navy and was usually home by 4 o'clock. He changed clothes, enjoyed a quick cup of coffee with my mother, and then he started working again. He always seemed to have some sort of project going on. He could fix anything, and my mother kept a running honey-do list for him. He did not really know how to relax much. Men worked, and that was that! Sunday was his day off, but we spent most of the day in church.

But today was Saturday, and in the month of November, that meant it was yardwork day! I was too little to actually help, but I could pick up small limbs and pine cones and then put them in the backyard on my father's burn pile. Since a 5-year-old has about a five-minute attention span, my work ethic lasted about that long. I would pick up a few pine cones and meander to the backyard, getting lost in my make-believe world several times before dropping the pine cones onto his burn pile.

My mother and my older sister were busy raking pine straw. Our large yard was filled with tall Florida pine trees, and in the fall when the cool weather rolled in, the pine trees rolled out a blanket of brown, prickly pine straw. It was everywhere!

And so autumn weather brought in raking, raking and more raking, leading to burning and more burning of all that pine straw!

My mother and sister would rake very methodically in long lines, raking in a big square. Once their straw line was too much for the rake, they piled it up in a big stack. My father would then come along with the wheelbarrow, load it up and take off for the backyard to dump it onto his burn pile.

Over and over again went the cycle. Rake, stack up, pick up, dump! Rake, stack up, pick up, dump!

Sound boring? Absolutely NOT!

Once the pine straw got to its stack-up stage, that's when I became the pine straw queen!

I would run over and jump on top of the piled-up straw. My father would continue to fill up his wheelbarrow with the brown needles, and when it was full he would pick me up and throw me on the top, only for me to roll around and giggle until I could finally get my little fingers on the metal sides and sturdy myself for the ride to the backyard. Once there, he would throw me onto the bigger pile that was to be burned later that day. Jumping back into the empty wheelbarrow, I would laugh and giggle my way back to the front yard, only to start the process all over again. I loved being daddy's pine straw queen!

After a long, fun-filled day of work, my mother would soak her dirty little girl in a warm bathtub and then pin curl her hair with bobby pins for church on Sunday.

Sitting in the tub, blowing bubbles through a wooden spool of thread, I could smell pine straw burning and hear my father raking and keeping the fire under control with the water hose.

It's been more than 60 years since I was the pine straw queen, but each time I smell pine burning, I'm there! Riding on a stack of pine straw in my daddy's wheelbarrow, a legend in my own mind!

I've read that of all the senses, the sense of smell outlasts all other memories. A smell is not only enough to relive a memory but is enough to actually pull out the rest of the memories with it.

I can look at the old faded picture of the chubby little tan girl riding in her father's wheelbarrow and smile. But just let me smell pine straw burning and once again I am rolling around in it, laughing with my father who smells like a mixture of Ivory soap, Old Spice shaving lotion, sweat and burning pine straw!

These memories are distant and fading but precious thoughts reminding me of my father's love for his little girl so long ago.

Psalm 139 reminds me of the constant and perfect love and knowledge of my Heavenly Father! He knows all my days from beginning to end, and I am forever safe in His perfect love!

"You formed my inward parts, You covered me in my mother's womb. I will praise You for I am fearfully and wonderfully made. Marvelous are Your works and that my soul knows very well. My frame was not

hidden from You when I was made in secret and skillfully wrought in the lowest part of the earth, Your eyes saw my substance being yet unformed and in Your book they all were written, the days fashioned for me, when as yet there were none of them. How precious also are Your thoughts to me, O God. How great is the sum of them, If I should count them they would be more in number than the sand. When I awake, I am still with you!" (Psalm 139:13-18)

13
Track Star

AS A LITTLE girl, it was hard to imagine my mother as anything other than my mother, especially as the baby in the family. By the time I arrived on the scene, mama was older than dirt, or so it seemed.

I was definitely not a planned pregnancy. My mother did jump up and scream when she found out the news she was expecting a baby, but not with joy! My parents lived through the Great Depression and World War II and were working hard, struggling to build a life within the scarcity of resources during that time. Their two children were finally growing up and the last thing she needed was a baby!

But she settled down to the reality and began the life of baby bottles and dirty diapers just at a time in her life when she was planning high school graduations and menopause. It wasn't the change of life she had expected. Motherhood again at age 40! Not her plan for middle-age, but there I was!

My parents were always older than most of the parents of my peers. It always embarrassed me that they were so old. My father was prematurely white-headed, and my friends thought he was my grandfather. My mother believed in living the plain and simple life and never gave any thought to cosmetics and hair dye. It was nonsense to her and so her gray hair, age spots and wrinkles were obvious to all, and she did not care a bit! As far as I was concerned, she was just plain ol' OLD!

But there were times when she would tell me stories about her younger days. I liked that. I especially enjoyed hearing about her high school days back in the late '20s! She was quiet and demure, studious and conscientious about her grades. I could certainly see that about her.

But then she would tell me stories about her athletic adventures of running TRACK! I just laughed at her ... the thought of my old mother running track? But she would unfold her stories like releasing a delicious present from its package and pull me into her daydreams of her past. I could see it clearly. She had a special way about telling stories. Her words of elocution would literally pull you into the experience with her!

She ran two events in track: the relay and the hurdles. I don't know which one she liked best, but she could spend a great amount of time describing each one. I think I liked to hear about the hurdles the best. She would stop whatever she was doing at the time and strike a serious pose—one hand held high and straight, her leg posed for takeoff like some Olympiad figure. She told of how important "the approach" was and the exact timing to stretch your leg up high and sail over the bars only to drop down securely on the track, pick up speed and quickly prepare for the next jump. Then with a twinkle in her eyes and glaring off into the distance, she would drift off into the memory and the glory of it all!

It was different with the relays. Relays were not about the

individual so much as the team. You had to be a team player. You had to learn how to pace your run, how to hold the baton, how to place it carefully in the next runner's hand. You had to know just when to let it go and then slowly stop running when you knew your team member was on his own lap. The win depended on each person doing their part for the good of the team!

I so enjoyed envisioning my mother young again—hard and strong, in gym shorts and a tank top, running and sweating and laughing and jumping up and down with her friends!

I would blink my eyes and the paradigm shifted. She was just my old mother again, washing dishes, folding clothes with her gray hair, age spots and wrinkles.

But now that's me—doing the dishes, folding the clothes—with my own gray hair, age spots and wrinkles; even though I try to cover them up, they are still there. It's the REAL me!

What will my children remember about their own mother? What stories will they tell to their children about their granny?

My mother taught me a lot more about running relays and jumping hurdles than she probably ever realized at the time.

In her old body, I saw strength of character. I saw strong legs of faith that carried her along the track of life. I saw the Lord lift her high over every hurdle she faced and let her sail along only long enough to gather strength for the next one with deeper faith and determination to continue to trust that her Lord would carry her on to victory.

I saw her soft, sweet hands hold tight the baton of God's word, holding it, pressing it to her bosom as she ran the relay of her own life. I saw her meet others along the way and pass the baton to them, gently laying it in their hand with just the right timing to let it go and then watch it produce strength of character and faith in their lives also.

I saw a childlike excitement in the way she loved her Heavenly Father. She knew He was watching for her at the finish line. He had given her everything she needed to finish the race down here. He sent His Son Jesus to give His life for hers at the cross of Calvary, forgiving her of all her sins and transferring His righteousness to her account and securing the goal she longed for that she knew she could never attain on her own … eternal life with God!

For sure, life is a test, a relay of sorts, full of hurdles, not to see if we pass the test but to teach us to keep believing in the only one who ever ran the race and won … Christ!

I found this old poem in one of my mother's Bibles. It was her life's resolve and has now become mine:

"My Resolution"
Annie Johnson Flint

I won't look back; God knows the fruitless efforts, the
wasted hours, the sinning, and the regrets;
I'll leave them all with Him, who blots the records, and
mercifully forgives and then forgets.
I won't look forward; God sees all the future, the road that
short or long, will lead me home.
And he will face with me its every trial, and bear with me
the burdens that may come,
But I'll look up … into the face of Jesus; For THERE my

heart can rest, my fears are stilled
And there is joy, and love, and light for darkness
And perfect peace and every hope fulfilled.

"For I am already being poured out as a drink offering, and the time of my departure is at hand. I have fought the good fight, I have finished the race, and I have kept the faith. Finally, there is laid up for me the crown of righteousness, which the Lord, the righteous Judge, will give to me on that Day, and not to me only, but also to all who have loved His appearing" (2 Timothy 4:6-8).

14
Parakeet and Providence

SITTING IN THE car with my father, he turned toward me with a solemn look and said, "Thea, this is a very big responsibility. Are you sure you are up to it?"

"Yes, yes, daddy, I'm sure!"

Jumping out of our big, old Oldsmobile, I ran toward the front door of the aviary.

For the past several weeks I had been going along with my mother while she visited one of her prayer group friends who was recovering from surgery. At first I did NOT want to go and tried every excuse I could think of to avoid going with her, but all that changed the first time I walked into Ms. Sally's house.

Ms. Sally had a beautiful parakeet named Tweetie Bird. He could talk AND do tricks!

I always loved animals, along with lizards, frogs, bugs, turtles and anything else I could find to drag home from the woods near our house. But none of them were like Ms. Sally's parakeet. I was in love!

Ms. Sally really loved her little parakeet. She treated him like her baby because she bought him when he was just a little tiny baby bird from a place called an aviary. My mother told me that was a place that raised birds.

I looked forward to each one of my mother's visits with Ms. Sally, but then she got well. No more visits with Tweetie Bird.

I began begging my parents for a parakeet. Not just any kind of parakeet would do, but a baby parakeet just like Ms. Sally's.

Finally, they succumbed to my constant pleadings and obtained the address of the aviary from Ms. Sally, and now I was sitting in the car with my father to go pick out my very own parakeet from all the young birdies! I was so excited I could hardly stand it!

Silently, I walked very slowly around each cage and looked at every bird. It had to be just the right one! Finally, I spied him. He was baby blue and white. He was smaller than Ms. Sally's bird. He looked right into my eyes, and I'm sure I heard him whisper, "Thea, take me, take me!" And so we did.

While my father paid the lady in front and bought a nice cage, I leaned ever so close to him, and whispered back, "I promise to love you and take care of you all of your life! You are my very own little baby blue birdie!"

I was exhilarated and got busy training my new pet! He would come to me when I called his name or when I clapped my hands. He would sit on my finger and kiss me. He also liked to sit on top of my head and scratch around in my hair, but what he loved most of all was to fly to my glass, sit on the edge and drink water.

I could hardly wait to get home from school each day to play with my new little baby bird. He was the talk of the town around our neighborhood, and all my friends liked to come over and play with him, too.

He especially liked my best friend, Tina. I think it was because she had long, thick blonde hair that he could REALLY scratch around in! Tina had six other brothers and sisters who were also playing somewhere in our neighborhood. At dinnertime I could hear her mom, Ms. Thelma, calling all the kids home.

Late one afternoon I heard the call … and Tina flew out the front door!

I could see it happen right before my eyes! My baby bird, that had been scratching in Tina's thick blonde hair, flew up toward the sky as soon as the screen door slammed shut!

"Stop, Tina, stop!" But she already realized what had happened and we both started crying. My little birdie just disappeared!

My precious baby blue parakeet had flown the coop! Literally.

I cried, I clapped, I called his name. My mother and father clapped, they called his name, but no baby blue bird was to be found.

I was devastated. My mother told me that the blue jays in the woods behind our house would take care of him. I did not think so because they were always mean to the other birds that came to our bird feeder each day. And after all … I promised … I told him I would take care of him forever.

Day after day I would come home from school, go out into the woods and call and clap for my little baby blue parakeet. Often, I would sit down in the pine straw and cry and pray that God would take care of my little baby bird.

Finally, my mother convinced me to get another parakeet—a green one this time. But my heart would always belong to my baby blue bird.

I still live near those woods of my childhood and sometimes as I drive by, I think of my little baby blue parakeet that stole my "little girl" heart.

It's funny that my husband and I both grew up in Beach Haven only four blocks from one other and never met! We both played in those same woods but our paths never crossed.

Neither one of us ever dreamed we would come back to the place where we grew up, but when his mother passed away, we decided to purchase the house of his childhood.

One hot summer night, we were relaxing in our pool in the backyard, enjoying a full moon, floating back and forth in the cool water and talking about our Beach Haven childhood memories. He began recounting the amazing story of a blue parakeet that flew through their open screen door at dinner time, frantically flapping its wings, and then perched on the edge of his father's iced tea glass and began to drink!

I couldn't believe what I was hearing! I was speechless! I just listened as he unfolded the story of the little blue parakeet that flew in his front door and became his pet. They bought him a cage and kept him for as long as he lived!

By this time, I was almost in tears! How could this be?

Because God cared … God saw.

He answered the prayer of a frantic little girl whose heart was broken. Sitting alone in the woods on a pile of pine straw, praying for her lost little bird, He sent him to a warm and loving home that belonged to the husband she would have 29 years in the future!

And when did I hear about God's answer to my prayer? That night in the pool would have been 40-plus years!

Coincidence, you say? No!

I say it's the providence of a loving God!

God's always at work, even though you may have to wait a long time or possibly never see His answers. But always remember that He knows, He hears, He cares and He always knows what's best!

Just trust Him … He is amazing!

"Are not two sparrows sold for a penny? And not one of them will fall to the ground apart from your Father. But even the hairs of your head are all numbered. Fear not, therefore; you are of more value than many sparrows. So everyone who acknowledges Me before men, I will also acknowledge before My Father who is in heaven. But whoever denies Me before men, I also will deny before My Father who is in heaven" (Matthew 10:29-33).

15
Waiting by the Seashore

"OH, MAMA, I want a really BIG one!"

Impatiently standing at the edge of the kitchen stool, I watched my mother stand tippy-toe on the stool seat to reach the highest shelf in her pantry.

"I really need a big one, mama, the biggest you've got!"

"Be patient, Thea!"

Patience was not one of my virtues.

It was summer time! It was hot, and my friends and I were getting ready to go to the beach with my mom and her best friends, Ms. Thelma and Ms. Susie.

As still as I could possibly be, I watched mama reach to the highest shelf of her pantry and carefully pull down a wide-mouth quart mason jar. "This will do just fine," she said.

"Oh, mama, couldn't you find one bigger than this?"

"No, that is big enough for a little girl like you. Now, go get a towel so you can wrap it up so you won't break it."

Off I run to the bathroom, lift the curtain that covered the shelves where my mom hid our sheets and towels, and grab a thinning white bath towel.

Running the towel to my mother in the kitchen, we carefully wrapped the quart jar, and packed it at the bottom of a large brown paper grocery bag she had waiting for me.

I was ready to go … actually, "antsy" to go, as my mom always said about me. I was antsy and fidgety! I think that meant I was always on "ready" and being still was almost impossible for the chubby little tan girl. Like I said, patience was definitely not one of my virtues!

After we packed my brown paper grocery bag with peanut butter and jelly sandwiches and a small jar filled with red Kool-Aid, we were finally ready to go!

I lived in Florida, and in the summer with no air conditioning, you lived outside most of the time, in hopes of catching a cool breeze. Fortunately, we lived near the beach, so that's where we spent most of the summer.

Stopping first at Ms. Susie's house next door, we picked up Petey, then down to Ms. Thelma's to pick up her gang of seven kids. We were ALL antsy by this time!

Finally, at the end of our road, the big brood of Beach Haven heathens threw open the front gate at Granddaddy Brown's and ran like crazy through his big yard and down the hill to our beach.

The beach really wasn't "ours" but all of us kids thought it was! This road, this beach, these people—we all belonged to each other! We didn't know life any other way. Granddaddy Brown originally owned all the land on the road where we lived, and through the years he became everyone's granddaddy, although he really belonged to Ms. Thelma's kids.

My mom and her friends sat down on a big log by the water's edge and began their grown-up talk with a few warnings that we better be nice to one another. By this time, we were all eating our sandwiches and digging around in our brown paper bags for our fishing gear!

No fishing poles, no hooks, no stinky bait, just wide-mouth jars and the leftover crust from our peanut butter sandwiches!

We were going … bread jugging!

It was one of our favorite pastimes! Bread jugging kept us busy for hours while our moms talked and laughed about who knows what.

We were busy … and we were serious about our daily catch! Why, maybe if we get some really big ones, our moms might let us keep them for pets!

All along the shoreline were little tan kids hovering over their jugs in the water … watching and waiting.

The idea was to use a piece of leftover bread crust, put it in a jar that was full of water and then carefully lay the jar on its side, underwater, near the shoreline. Then, all you had to do was to stand over your jug, very still, and wait for the minnows to get curious and swim innocently into your trap. Then, "quick as a wink," as my mama said, you could jerk up the jar and "lo and behold," you have yourself a minnow! And each of us vowed to catch more minnows than our friends!

But then, what did we do with all our minnows?

We had that covered. Each child dug a deep hole and filled it up with salty bayou water, just waiting to be filled with the catch of the day!

The older kids ran to the end of the pier and did cannon balls into the deep end. The big kids liked to "roughhouse," as my mama said. But us little kids loved bread jugging!

After a couple of hours, most of us had at least one or two minnows in our holding tanks, and we were "proud as peacocks," as my mama said! But finally our moms would stand up and holler, "Get your stuff kids, we're going home."

That was our cue to start begging: "Please let us take our fish home … we could keep them in our glass jar and feed them bread crumbs every day!" "No", they said. We were told to "put them back in the water so they can swim home to their mama that lives under the Brown's pier." Sorrowfully, we scooped out our minnows and released them on the shoreline. Funny, some of them didn't move. I guess they were tired.

I have so many fond memories of playing at the beach during the summertime with my neighborhood buddies. Sometimes we floated around in our old black inner tube tires and sang songs we'd learned in school; other times we built elaborate sandcastles with long, deep moats and then sat down and waited for the tide to roll in and fill the moat until it overflowed. I loved the beach! My mama said that at the end of the summer, I was as "brown as a berry." I thought berries were red or purple, but I guess mama knew what she was talking about!

After I became an adult and moved back to Pensacola, I enjoyed spending time with my parents. They still lived in the same house where I grew up, the house near the beach. I loved going back to my old Beach Haven homestead, sitting down at the dining room table, drinking a cup of coffee and just chatting. My parents had so much wisdom to share, and as an adult, I was finally eager to drink from their well.

My mother loved God's Word and she loved to pray … and I loved to hear her pray! There was no doubt she had a personal relationship with the Lord, and she prayed all the time. One time, she told me that to her prayer was like being a small child, sitting on the shoreline of the beach, digging a little hole and then waiting for the power of the whole ocean to come fill it up!

Immediately, I could identify. I remembered the chubby little tan girl sitting at the shoreline of the Beach Haven bayou. My mother said we dig our holes by making requests that are "according to God's will," which we learn by reading the Bible, and then we wait and believe that the same God that created the water in all the oceans will certainly fill up our little hole with whatever is necessary for our life. He created us and certainly knows what's best for us. We just need to enjoy being little and rest in His bigness! Her faith was pure and simple but not simplistic—it was deep and rich and full of wisdom from above.

One of my mother's favorite verses in the Bible is found in Psalm 119:49-50: "Remember Your Word to your servant upon which You have caused me to hope. This is my comfort in my affliction. For Your Word has given me life."

Sitting around the dining room table with my aging parents, I saw strength and wisdom. They'd survived two world wars, the Great Depression, multiple losses, including the deaths of twin boys, both parents, sisters, and brothers, as well as financial losses and many sorrows in assorted situations, but they were still peaceful, strong, courageous and happily married. So many people of their generation claimed to be self-made men, but not my parents. They had ONE hope ... ONE source of strength and life: God and His Holy Word!

They are both gone now, but their memory and their example live within me. I follow their path. I, too, sit by the seashore each day, digging my little hole, placing God's promises there. I enjoy being "little" and I rest in His Holy Word, the only true source of hope and life!

"So shall My Word be that goes forth from My mouth; it shall not return to Me void, but it shall accomplish what I please, and it shall prosper in the thing I send it" (Isaiah 55:11).

"O Lord, how manifold are Your works! In wisdom You have made them all. The earth is full of Your possessions, this great and wide sea, in which are innumerable teeming things, living things both small and great. These all wait for You that You may give them their food in due season. What You give them, they gather in; You open your hand, they are filled with good" (Psalm 104:24-25, 27-28).

"Now this is the confidence that we have in Him, that if we ask anything, according to His will, He hears us. And if we know that He hears us, whatever we ask, we know that we have the petitions that we have asked of Him" (1 John 5:14-15).

16
A Smile in the Dark

SNEAKING OUT OF the house, I ran as fast as I could to the big wooden trailer parked on the side of our yard. It was just starting to rain, and my mother thought I was playing inside the house. She and her neighbor friend, Ms. Thelma, were having coffee so she was unaware I'd slipped away.

I was wearing my favorite overalls. It was a cold day; nevertheless, I was snuggly warm. I loved these overalls. My mother told me they were like the ones the railroad conductors wore. I wanted to be a railroad conductor one day! My mother would read to me each night from one of my Little Golden Books, and one of my favorite stories was "The Little Engine That Could." I also wanted to be that little engine one day!

I would giggle as she recited the little engine's words as he climbed up a steep hill: "I think I can, I think I can, I think I can." Then peaking at the top of the hill, the little engine laughed as it raced down the hill: "I thought I could, I thought I could, I thought I could!"

Today I was the conductor AND the little engine! "I think I can get to the wagon ... I think I can, I think I can!"

Running as fast as my chubby little legs would carry me, I

stopped at the edge of the wagon and then crawled under as far as I could to get out of the rain.

Crossing my legs Indian style (I also wanted to be an Indian princess one day!), I sat very quietly and listened. Nothing but the sound of the rain falling softly on the wagon above me. I must have pulled off my great escape—I was safe, at least for now.

Crawling out from underneath the wooden trailer, I began pulling myself up on one of the tires. Straining to get to the top of the wheel, I could see the big black tarp. I knew what was under the tarp, and I couldn't wait to get there!

Looking toward the house again, I felt relieved in my freedom. My mother still did not realize I was missing!

Slowly I lifted the heavy black tarp and crawled into the back of the trailer. Pulling the heavy tarp back over my head, I settled down just in the nick of time.

It started pouring down rain, "like cats and dogs," as my mother used to say. But that made it even better!

The chubby little tan girl loved to sneak away and be alone in her secret hideaways, and this was one of her favorite places!

My daddy's big wooden trailer was filled to the brim with oak leaves! He had just brought them home from one of his church friends, Mr. Lord, who had huge oak trees that seemed to have wings that covered his whole backyard with lots of leaves! We only had tall pine trees and pine straw everywhere. I don't know why my daddy wanted Mr. Lord's oak leaves, but often during the winter, my father would bring some oak leaves home in his big old wagon. I think I heard my mama say he wanted them for his garden. It didn't matter to the chubby little tan girl. I just loved to lie down in them and let the leaves cover my whole body except for my little round face! I loved to lie there very quiet, all covered up, my face staring up in the dark at the black tarp touching my nose.

I could feel the pelting of the rain on the tarp and hear the pitter-patter of the raindrops. It was like music to me. The leaves were soft and warm but smelled like the dirt of my daddy's garden. It was very dark except for a little light that would shine through the corners of the tarp.

Lying there, in my secret hideaway, my little mouth slowly turned its corners upward, and a big smile covered my face!

But the ecstasy only lasted a few minutes before I heard the voice of reality calling me!

"Thea Judith Burge, you better get yourself in this house right this minute!"

Squirming out from under the tarp, I called back, "I'm coming," and ran to my mother, standing at the screen door with her hands on her hips! Stooping down, she dried off my chubby round face, dusted the leaves off and scooted me into the house.

In a tone that told me she did not really expect to find out, my mother uttered, "Where in the world has that child been?"

I was always running off somewhere to hide and play pretend.

I often think about the little girl smiling in the dark. She didn't realize all the years ahead of her that she would live in reality, hiding in the darkness.

And then, there was grace. The same unchanging, everlasting God, the One who created her, knew every day of her life before she ever was formed within her mother's womb, knew the good, the bad and the ugly of her life, He had a plan! As the chubby little tan girl came running when she heard her mother's voice, she would eventually hear another voice and she would come running — He was calling her out of her darkness to live in the light of God!

And then one day, the little girl learned to pray.

She found a "secret place" where she could escape, a place that was peaceful and safe. Where the voices she heard were ones filled with love and forgiveness, with hope and peace. It was a place that was hidden and yet always available. A place where she could run to and tune out the world of sight and rest in the unseen reality of faith and hope in God alone.

She loved going there. To the secret place of prayer with God. It felt so wonderful to finally be real — there were no secrets in the secret place. No surprises in the secret place because God already knows it all. The little chubby girl knew she was truly known in the secret place; no more wishing she could be someone else when she grew up. She was seen by a Father who loved her before the foundations of the world, loved her when she was in darkness, and He brought her to live with Him in the light. "For God, who said, 'Let light shine out of darkness,' has shone in our hearts to give the light of the knowledge of the Glory of God in the face of Jesus Christ" (2 Corinthians 4:6). She listened to Him as she read from His book, the Bible. His words were real and powerful; they became her source of truth and life. She loved Him, she loved His Word, she loved the secret place of prayer with Him.

"Even to your old age and gray hairs I Am He, I Am He who will sustain you, I have made you and I will carry you; I will sustain you

and I will rescue you" (Isaiah 46:4).

"But when you pray, go into your room and shut the door, and pray to your Father who is in secret, and your Father who sees in secret will reward you" (Matthew 6:6).

So what was her reward? His presence, just being with Him. She's not the chubby little tan girl anymore, but still the corners of her mouth turn upward and a smile begins to cover her face! He is always enough to fill her heart with joy!

"One thing I have asked of the Lord and that I will seek; that I may dwell in the house of the Lord (in his presence) all the days of my life, to gaze upon the beauty (the delightful loveliness and majestic grandeur) of the Lord and to meditate in His temple"(Psalm 27:4 Amplified Bible).

"He who dwells in the secret place of the Most High shall abide under the shadow of the Almighty. I will say of the Lord, He is my refuge and my fortress, my God, in Him I will trust" (Psalm 91:1-2).

"In the time of trouble, He shall hide me in His pavilion; in the secret place of His Tabernacle He shall hide me; He shall set me on a rock" (Psalm 27:5).

17
Slime, Swamps and the Slippery Slope

"BE CAREFUL," I hollered over my shoulder to my friends following me. "It's really slippery!"

Looking down at my bare feet through several inches of yellow swamp water, I slowly edged forward on the long, slimy log. I could see the other side of the pond at the end of the dead pine tree lying in the swampy water. I decided this tree would be the perfect bridge for me and my friends to use to get to the other side of the swampy pond.

I heard one of my younger neighborhood buddies whimpering, "Thea, I'm afraid—there might be snakes out here!" Screaming over my shoulder again, I hollered back, "Of course there are snakes out here, but don't be such a chicken! I've got my daddy's knife. I'll just kill 'em!"

The chubby little tan girl was a "knife-packing" 10-year-old—a legend in her own mind!

My daddy's tool shed was in the back of our house and one day while nosing around, I found an old rusty pocketknife in one of the drawers. I took it! I could hardly open it because of the rust, but just holding it in my hand made me feel invincible! Oh yes, the chubby little tan girl was prepared to take on ALL kinds of wild animals with this knife, especially snakes. Just like my big brother!

My brother, Sonny, was 17 years older than me. He left to join the military when I was a toddler, and I have no recollection of ever living with him. But I knew all the fantastic stories about my older brother. To the chubby little tan girl, he was almost like Superman! I was convinced Sonny had superpowers, and he had a special fondness for snakes! He collected them and kept them in one of his bureau drawers in his bedroom, much to my grandmother's surprise who found them when she was putting away his folded clothes!

When my parents first moved to Beach Haven it was just palmettos, pine trees, scrub oaks and red clay paths. My parents were thrilled to finally buy property where they could build their own home. It was going to take time and a lot of hard work, but building a home was their dream and "hard work never hurt anyone," a phrase I often heard from my mother.

It was right after the war, a time when life was hard and people were too! My big brother had his first paper route when he was only 12 and never stopped working. My mother often told me that whatever money he made, he gave to her to help pay the bills. My daddy held down two and sometimes three jobs to make ends meet. But at night and on weekends, my daddy and my big brother built our house in Beach Haven. Even my 5-year-old sister did her part by hammering nails straight again so they could be reused. Everyone worked hard, and the house was finally completed by the "sweat of their brow," as my mama said!

All I really knew about my big brother was from the stories I was told. My sister was 10 years older than me, and she and my parents talked about my brother a lot, especially when he was away in the military. My sister was always really good to me. But when she started having boyfriends, she didn't laugh when I teased her. One night she got really mad at me when I slipped a roach under her sheets. Oh well, I guess that's just sisters!

But my big brother was another story.

When they moved out to Beach Haven, he was 13 years old and my sister was 5. Beach Haven was raw, a whole world of unexplored territory! My big brother was always one to "live on the edge." I often heard tales about his escapades.

My favorite story was about the day he was bitten by a water moccasin in the swamp near our home. You think he would rush home and get help, but he didn't! Superman big brother just took out his knife, cut a big X in his leg and sucked all the poison out! My mother was none the wiser, at least not until he confessed. I think after a while she didn't want to know what he was doing, so she just prayed a lot!

But hey, if he can do it, then I can do it too! Just let those water moccasins come after me … I'm ready!

Finally, making it to the end of the slippery tree—our bare feet covered in slime, our necks sweaty and adorned with dirt bead necklaces—the Beach Haven bandits were safe on the other side of the big swampy pond!

The chubby little tan girl, a foolish little girl once again! My mother often told me that God watched over children and fools—the look on her face when she said this told me what category I fell into that day!

"The way of the fool is right in his own eyes, but a wise man listens to advice" (Proverbs 12:15).

"O, God, you know my foolishness, and my guiltiness is not hidden from you" (Psalm 69:45).

My parents were always trying to protect me and guide me in the right direction; it seems like most of my life I was pulling to go the other way! I had places to go and things to do!

Life in Beach Haven could be dangerous back when I was a little girl! But a different kind of dangerous. Parents didn't worry about someone stealing us when we were playing by ourselves in the woods or down at the beach. It didn't cross their mind because it didn't happen. Life was different. We were given freedoms pretty early in life to explore our surroundings by ourselves. It was fun but could also be very dangerous.

I remember one day my mother found a rattlesnake curled up in our backyard; my father killed it with his shovel. He also showed me the red hourglass shape on the belly of a black widow spider he'd just killed in one of the drawers in his tool shed (yes, the same drawers I was nosing around in). Early one morning, my mother found a scorpion in a shoe she was about to put on!

I'll never forget the day one of the neighbors caught a shark under the same pier I swam under day after day in the summertime! All of these dangers the Beach Haven bandits were protected from. One bite and our lives could have been forever changed, but weren't!

We continued playing on the beach by ourselves, building forts in our woods with knives and axes and wading in grassy swamp marshes, walking on slimy, slippery dead trees, never even thinking about the dangers that lurked there: poisonous snakes, black widow and brown recluse spiders, scorpions, sharks and foolishness in general! Sometimes I shudder to think of all that could have happened to us, but didn't, while we roamed around in our freedom! Thank you, Lord!

I am so blessed to be a senior citizen who still lives near the same Beach Haven neighborhood where I grew up. I walk the same beach and reminisce about all the wonderful times I had as the chubby little tan girl. When I walk past the swampy pond, I laugh at my younger self—she was a handful of princess pride!

Thinking of my life as an adult, I also shudder to think of what could have happened, but didn't. Many times I've been protected by the hand of a gracious and merciful God to a foolish woman who should have known better, but didn't.

I am also blessed and privileged to be the child that spent the most time with my parents as an adult. They affected me or should I say "infected" me, with their love and passion for the Lord and His Holy Word.

As a little girl I thought I knew everything, and they knew nothing. That mind-set continued for many years but thankfully, by God's grace, He opened my eyes and ears to see them and hear them with a new desire to learn. I listened as a disciple would. They taught; I listened and I followed. I am still listening and learning from them as I continue to remember how they followed Jesus the Lord for the glory of God the Father.

In all of life, we are learning. We're greatly influenced by people and experiences, both good and bad. How we react to life tends to make us bitter or better as the years take their toll on our lives. My little-girl immaturity was finally shattered, and I realized there is NO Superman and there ARE a lot of scary things out there just waiting to drain the life from us, and it's foolish to walk the slippery slope of sin … it's not worth the temporary thrill!

My parents were not perfect by any means, but I trusted them. They were people of their word, and they were people of the Word, the Bible.

And so, like them, I follow the trail they paved before me. Their lives marked out a well-worn path of surrender to God and obedience to the Bible through a sweet and ongoing personal relationship with Jesus. I realize that not all people follow the same path, but I don't trust all people. I trusted my parents and they said, "Thea, this is the way of truth." I believed them, and I followed.

"My son, do not forget my law, but let your heart keep my commands; for length of days and long life and peace it will add to you. Let not mercy and truth forsake you; bind them around your neck, write them on the tablets of your heart. And so find favor and high esteem in the sight of God and man. Trust in the Lord with all your heart, and lean not to our own understanding, in all your ways acknowledge Him and He shall direct your paths. Do not be wise in your own eyes, fear the Lord and depart from evil, it will be health to your flesh and strength to your bones" (Proverbs 3:1-8).

"Hear my children, the instruction of a father, and give attention to know understanding; for I give you good doctrine; do not forsake my law" (Proverbs 4:1-2). "But the path of the just is like the shining sun that shines ever brighter unto the perfect day" (Proverbs 4:18). "Jesus answered, 'I am the WAY and the TRUTH and the LIFE. No one comes to the Father except through Me'" (John 14:6).

18
Happy Father's Day, Daddy

AS I SHUFFLED down the hallway into the bathroom after I woke, I saw him out of the corner of my eye. Sitting in my grandmother's old maple rocking chair with a Bible in his lap, staring out the open front door, was my father. His hair was snow white, almost glowing as the morning sun shone into our living room. As he sat and slowly rocked and read his Bible, my mother was busy down the hall in the kitchen.

I could smell bacon and coffee and (I think) blueberry pancakes. It was Saturday morning in the fall, and I was in my late teens.

My father had changed over the last several years, or maybe it was me who had changed. But that day, he looked different to me — there was a softness about him. I watched him read and stare out the front door; he was oblivious to me penetrating his quiet time.

If you were fortunate to have lived with parents who stuck it out and did not divorce, you realized that your parents were just human. They made mistakes, they didn't know everything you thought they should know, and they were not as strong as you once thought … and oftentimes they changed as they got older.

My parents had three children in three different generations. My older brother was 17 years my senior, and my sister, 10 years. I was their "surprise package."

If you are the first child, you knew the young parent, and you were their experiment child. Parenting doesn't come with instructions, it's on-the-job training! They have young bodies, big ideas and lots of energy but can be overconfident in themselves and sometimes foolish, even though they don't always realize it. You received all their attention and probably grew up with leadership qualities, or so they say (whoever THEY are)!

If you are the middle child, you knew the maturing parent. They were beginning to realize that things hadn't materialized the way they had hoped. This was usually the time of building: homes, careers, lifestyles. And along with all the building comes problems with lack of time, energy, money and sometimes too much family! It can be a time of drama and second children tend to be peacemakers.

If you are the baby in the family, you knew the older, weaker parents. By the time you came around, they had lived long enough to experience some pain and actually live through it. Hopefully they gained some wisdom from their problems and became better, not bitter.

Being human means having problems, and having problems means having pain. I read somewhere that pain is not optional but misery is.

If you are the baby in the family, you may be the one who really gets to know the older parent, who has learned that misery is optional and that joy and contentment is a gift from God, apart from anything else!

I was born to two "menopausal" parents! My father already had white hair when I was born and it wasn't just "light blond" as he used to tell me.

He would often comment that it was a shame that young bodies were wasted on young men because when you finally learn how to live, your body is usually getting ready to die! Of course, he would chuckle when he said that. But as I stared at him that early Saturday morning sitting in my grandmother's rocking chair, reading his Bible, staring out the front door, lost in thought, I knew he was different. He was older, weaker, softer, wiser and contented. He was looking upward to God and His Word, not so much at his own sufficiency or circumstances anymore.

I was different too. I was finally beginning to realize a few elementary things about love, life and my parents. Just about the time I was ready to leave home, I wanted to stay and be their little girl again—gentle and easy, not strong-willed and rebellious!

The two people I tried to pull away from were really the two people who loved me the most, and now I was getting ready to leave them and launch out into my adult life.

I watched my dad on that early Saturday morning look down at his Bible and read awhile, then look out to our beautiful manicured front yard that he so meticulously cared for. I could see his eyelids close. I knew he was praying.

With his eyes closed, he was staring up at the God he knew, gazing at a city he would go to one day, content to live in a Presence that was invisible but that enveloped him in sweetness and joy.

"Blessed is the man who walketh not in the counsel of the ungodly nor stands in the path of sinners nor sits in the seat of the scornful. But his delight (the blessed man) is in the law of the Lord (the Bible) and in His law he meditates day and night. And he shall be like a tree, planted by the rivers of water that yields its fruit in its season, and its leaf does not wither and whatever he does shall prosper" (Psalm 1:1-3).

That day in my late teens, I stared at a man who knew God. Oh, I knew "about" his God as my parents took me to church my entire life, but until I left home, I did not have a personal relationship with the God my father and mother knew. But I knew my dad; I knew he loved me. He had forgiven me of all the misery I had caused them and he really did want only the best for me, even though he may not have known how to get that across to his strong-willed baby girl.

I watched him seek the Lord, and I saw him change—and I changed also … in time.

God planted my dad by the rivers of water, and he drank deeply and brought forth fruit—love, joy, peace and contentment—in his season, the season of old age, and I was the blessed child to have known the man of old age.

He never really knew how much his life of faith affected me. He died when I was only 27. I left home at 19, had my own salvation experience with God at 21, and returned to Pensacola at 24. We only had three short years to enjoy each other as adults, adopted by God, into the family of God, through the blood of Christ. He was my earthly father but my spiritual brother in Christ.

He stayed very busy in his retired life, enjoying being with his wife of almost 50 years, doing a little traveling, some fishing, working at the church and getting to enjoy being a grandpa to my 2-year-old son. It was a very short few years, but they were wonderful. Our relationship was the best it had ever been! He was lighthearted and joyful. We had many conversations about the Lord over coffee at the dining room table. And then he was gone.

One Sunday he was serving communion at church; the next Sunday he suffered a major heart attack and entered into the rest of the Lord. He was only 66, and according to his doctors, was in excellent health. But what did THEY know? It was God's timing, not the doctors'. He left us … but not completely.

His life is still bearing luscious fruit in my life. I remember him with enormous gratitude. I remember the morning I peered into his quiet time and he reminds me to "go deep," to look up to God, to look deep into God's Word, to take the time to meditate on it—to pray, to praise and be grateful, to love, to serve others joyfully and just ENJOY life … savor each moment!

I know I will see him one day, but until then, thank you, daddy! I love you!

"Jesus answered, 'I am the WAY and the TRUTH and the LIFE. No one comes to the Father except through Me'" (John 14:6).

19
Red Clay Courage

THE AIR WAS thick and dusty on the red clay playground. Screams and shouts of little boys filled the air. Then all of a sudden, there was a hush and the boys froze in their tracks.

There he was, standing at least 10 feet tall, dressed in full military garb with his black high-top leather boots.

Julius Wright was the headmaster of the military school where the little third-grade boy had just started attending.

The little boy just stood there, his face hot with sweat and smeared with red clay, flushed from the fight with the other boy. They'd been rolling around on the hard, red clay, beating each other in the face, their fight only perpetuated by the screams of all the other boys that encircled them.

Scared to even breathe, much less say anything, he just fixed his eyes on the headmaster.

After it seemed like five minutes of silence, Mr. Wright asked, "Who started this?" Silence … he asked again and looked around the circle of sweaty little third-grade boys.

Finally, one of the boys in the circle said, quietly, "It wasn't Johnny; it was the other boy."

The headmaster then looked at the little boy named Johnny and asked, "What happened?" Little Johnny, still frozen in his tracks, just looked at him with tears streaming down his flushed face and said nothing.

The snitch spoke up again and said, "It was because he was calling him names and making fun of the way he talks."

The headmaster knew about little Johnny Burge. His parents had enrolled him in military school this year because he had a history of run-ins with other boys bullying him. They hoped it would be different at Wright's Military Academy.

It wasn't. And here he was again, his sweaty little face, his jaw jutted out, his eyes set like steel with tears running down his face, his tender heart bleeding again.

Mr. Wright took a moment to size up the situation, then looked straight at little Johnny Burge and said, "I guess you need to finish what was started." The fight resumed, and then with one hit to the other little boy's nose, he stepped into his manhood. No one would bully little Johnny Burge again!

My daddy stuttered … really bad.

I remember daddy telling me that story about Mr. Wright and the day he helped my daddy get his freedom back. My father was forever changed by that man, Headmaster Julius T. Wright. Daddy eventually graduated from Wright's Military Academy and when Mr. Wright passed away, he was asked to play "Taps" at his funeral. Daddy said he could hardly blow his horn because he was so filled with tears of respect, love and appreciation for that man.

Bullying has been around forever and will always continue, because it comes from the heart.

The Bible tells us that "the heart is deceitful above all things and desperately wicked; who can know it?" (Jeremiah 17:9). And then Proverbs 4:23 instructs, "We should guard our heart above all else, for it determines the course of our life." All of life is a heart thing!

Daddy was a man's man, but his heart was very tuned in to protect those who needed protection. He was tough, but he had a heart of wisdom that wanted to do right for the right reasons, and he set that example for all his children.

I remember as a kid, he gave me a set of boxing gloves with careful instructions not to fight; however, he also told me that if I was forced to fight, I should look them square in the eye and then hit them as hard as I could, right on their nose, right between their eyes. That sounded like fun to me! "Yes, daddy, I'll do just that!" No one would push me around! I remember setting up a boxing ring out in our front yard between four tall pine trees. I would wear my boxing gloves and pretend box with my neighborhood buddies. We picked out funny names for ourselves and hung towels around our necks and spit in our corner of the boxing ring! But it was just pretend. We liked to pretend a lot!

Because my daddy stuttered, he didn't talk much. My mother did most of the talking. But my daddy could speak volumes with just a look. And if he ever said my whole name without stuttering … "Thea Judith Burge!" … I was in deep trouble for sure! He used to call me the atomic bomb! I was born to my parents when they thought they were almost finished raising children, and I'm sure I wearied the middle-aged couple many times.

When I was about 6 years old, my older brother and his wife had the first grandchild, a beautiful little blond, blue-eyed boy,

John W. Burge V, and my daddy was "itching" to go see him! Surprisingly, there was a prayer retreat my mother wanted to attend on the same route to the new grandbaby's house, so daddy volunteered to drive.

At the prayer conference, the gospel was preached, fellowship was sweet and at the end of the conference, they gathered around daddy in a circle of love, laid hands on him and prayed. A miracle happened.

My mother said my daddy went to their cabin, threw himself across the bed and cried like she had never seen him cry before. She said it was like a dam had opened up and torrents of tears exploded years of burdens and sin. She just sat there on the bed trying to comfort him. Finally, after he quit crying, he dried his tears and spoke to her for the first time without stuttering. There was a calmness in his speech he'd never had before. She said they sang hymns together in the car all the way home.

A slight stammer in his speech did return, but never the forceful and crippling stuttering he'd struggled with for more than 40 years!

A life changed within a different circle—not of war but of love.

My daddy taught me so many things without saying a word. I saw how hard he worked and I learned good work ethics. I saw how he loved my mother and always treated her with respect, and I learned what a good marriage looks like. I saw his faithfulness to serve the Lord in his church, and I learned what godly men look like. I saw how dependable he was, and I learned what commitment to your word looks like. I saw how honest he was with everything he did, and I learned the importance of being true to God first, then yourself and then to others.

Daddy only lived a few years after I became a true believer in Christ, but we enjoyed many rich times together, even if it was only a short time. My father loved me, although I seldom heard those words from him. My daddy was proud of me, although he didn't say it often. His caring look to me spoke volumes, and when he would smile his squinty-eyed smile, my heart was elated!

I still have an old yellowed piece of paper with his signed words, "I love you, daddy." They were written more than 40 years ago. I can take one look at his handwriting and tears start rolling again. Love goes on forever. Today is my daddy's birthday. He would have been 104! Happy birthday, daddy, and thank you for everything! I love you and miss you terribly!

20
Mattress Time

OPENING THE REFRIGERATOR door, I reached for the milk carton. With one hand full of oatmeal-raisin cookies, I poured myself a large glass of cold milk. I loved milk and cookies. Then I heard it, a faint noise at the end of the hallway. I moved slowly toward the sound.

Stepping down into the dining room, I finally made it out. It was my mother … crying.

Earlier at school that day, I had been called to the principal's office. My mother was there. Previously caught for passing notes in my eighth-grade history class, I knew what was coming. My note explained in great detail my escapades at my girlfriend's house when her mom was not at home the previous weekend. My detailed account, scattered and punctuated with swear words, lay on the principal's desk. All the swear words were circled in red ink. I was in deep trouble. Caught again! It was not a pretty picture.

I sat in his office, solemn faced, listening to the scolding and warnings from the principal. I just watched my mother. She sat there motionless and listened to his every word. She never once looked at me.

"No," she said. She did not need to read the note; she trusted what he said was true.

She got up from her chair, politely told him thank you, shook his hand, and then said, "Let's go home."

I followed her out to our big old car. We always had big old cars. My mother reminded me of a child when she sat behind the wheel. She was a very small woman. She could hardly see over the steering wheel.

There were few words on the drive home, and that made me even more uneasy. I knew what was going down. I'd been here before. She would talk to my daddy when he got home from work, then they would decide what to do. I knew there would be restrictions of some sort. If you do the crime, you will do the time! I was guilty, but I thought it was worth it. My father always said, "Thea, if you don't listen, then you have to feel." The restrictions would be annoying, but I learned how to endure them until I would get my freedom back again!

But today was different somehow.

Their bedroom door was slightly ajar. Quietly, I stood there with my cookies and milk and watched her.

There she was, my tiny little mother, kneeling next to her bed. Her head was buried in the mattress and she was crying … sobbing, actually. I could see her whole body shaking.

Standing there watching her, I thought to myself, "She's nuts … a real religious fanatic!"

Then, nonchalantly, I went to my room, closed the door and feasted on my cookies and milk, oblivious of her pain or the depth of her love for me.

Each time that memory flashes through my mind, it reminds me of the hardness of the human heart—the hardness of my own heart—and the grace of God through the prayers of a godly mother.

Oh, I had gone to church my whole life and I could have told you all the right words to say if you are a Christian, but I wasn't one. Having godly parents and going to church doesn't make you a Christian. That one point in time is like an indelible photo in my memory. It reminds me of God's grace to one rebellious dead girl, ME!

As I entered high school, I wised up a bit and decided life was more fun if I stayed out of trouble and made better grades. After all, in just a few more years, I would be on my own and could do whatever I wanted to. I would not have to live by their rules or their religion!

After all, everyone has a right to their own opinions, don't they? My answer was a definite YES!

Years passed and God answered my mother's prayers. I came to know the Lord in a personal way when I was 21 years old, alone, on my knees in the downstairs of a basement apartment in Denver, Colorado.

But I wonder how much "mattress time" my mom did for me? How many times did she bury her face in the pillow and fill it with tears? How often did she turn her head into the mattress at night and cry so my daddy could not hear her and silently pray, "Lord, save Thea, heal Thea as only You can. I trust You. I will never stop asking, Lord. You alone are her answer for life!"

Whenever I write these little stories about my mother, it's to glorify God for His amazing grace that saved a wretch like me, and to appreciate the little woman who gave me life (physically) and then took me in prayer to the only One who could give me life spiritually, my Savior, the Lord Jesus Christ!

"But you, being dead in your trespasses and the uncircumcision of your flesh, He has made alive together with Him, having forgiven you all your trespasses, having wiped out the hand writing of requirements that was against us, which was contrary to us. And He has taken it out of the way, having nailed it to the cross" (Colossians 2:13-14).

"But God, being rich in mercy, because of the great love with which He loved us, even when we were dead in our trespasses, made us alive together with Christ, by grace have you been saved and raised us up with Him and seated us with Him in the heavenly places in Christ Jesus, so that in the coming ages He might show the immeasurable riches of His grace in kindness toward us in Christ Jesus. For by grace you have been saved through faith. And this is NOT your own doing; it is the gift of God, not of works, so that no one may boast" (Ephesians 2:4-9).

"I thank God, whom I serve from my forefathers with pure conscience, that without ceasing I have remembrance of thee in my prayers day and night" (2 Timothy 1:3).

21
Window to the Soul

WAKING UP, I found myself standing alone in a dark tunnel. I felt the darkness closing in around me, like arms of steel crushing against the sides of my body. I could hardly breathe; my heart raced and I tried to take a deep breath. This wall of darkness pushed at my back and moved me forward into a long, dark hallway.

There was a small ray of light above me, slightly illuminating what was ahead. I saw a narrow hall with closed doors on each side. I slowly moved toward the first door on my left. I grabbed the handle and pulled, twisting right and left. Nothing. It remained locked. I moved to the next door and grabbed again. Nothing … nothing but darkness surrounded me, even though I could see the small flicker of light hovering over my head. I took a few more steps forward and reached for the handle of the next door on my right. It moved and I pushed it forward slightly. Instantly, light burst toward me and I quickly moved into the room.

Closing the door behind me, I finally felt safe. I leaned my body against the closed door, closed my eyes and enjoyed the feeling. Tilting my head upward, I could feel the warmth of the brightness. It felt like sunshine on my face on a beautiful Florida day in the springtime.

I smelled a faint aroma of gardenia blossoms and I remembered how they used to grow next to my parents' bedroom window. My heart settled as I thought of my parents. I began to feel safe.

Slowly I opened my eyes and looked around. It took a minute for my eyes to adjust to the brightness, but then I began to see clearly. I was in a beautiful bedroom. It was bright and cheerful. The walls were painted buttercup yellow with white baseboards and crown molding. There on the wall in front of me was a large double-wide window. It was open, and I could smell freshly cut grass.

The window was dressed with beautiful, white frilly curtains that were waving in the breeze from outside. They seemed to beckon me to the window. I moved toward it and peered outside. It was glorious. A beautiful day. The sky was blue like the Caribbean Sea with full, fluffy clouds like cotton balls dancing around. I could hear birds chirping and watched a beautiful red cardinal perch on the branch of a large oak tree next to the window. The grass had been freshly cut and it was brilliant green like a golf course. It smelled clean and fresh. Patches of colorful flowers caught my eye: pansies, daffodils and tulips. It smelled and felt like springtime. It was intoxicating!

At the top of one of the hills there was a bright, shiny swing set. No one was on it, but the swing was slowly moving back and forth in the breeze. It was lovely. I wanted to push myself through the window and go run and play outside.

But something was keeping me in the room.

Something or someone said, "Turn around. Tell me what you see."

Slowly I turned around and looked, and there she was: alone on a big bed with a ruffled bedspread sat a little girl.

The bedspread was yellow and white gingham check with white eyelet pillows scattered around. There was a worn brown teddy bear resting beside some Little Golden Books opened on the bed. It was all so simple and yet beautiful. My eyes could hardly take it all in—the brightness, the smells, the birds, the beauty, the peace and the bed, especially the bed. A feeling of love settled over me as I gazed upon the bed with the little girl sitting there. I sensed there was something very special about her.

She appeared to be about 3 or 4 years old and oblivious to me being in the room with her. She was just sitting on her bed, entertaining herself, lying down pretending like she was reading to her teddy bear from her Little Golden Books. I could hear her singing a little song to herself. I couldn't understand the words, but the tune seemed vaguely familiar. She was lost in the joy of her make-believe world.

I was spellbound. Unable to move, I just watched her, frozen in time.

And then all of a sudden, she stopped singing. She looked up, and her big brown eyes caught mine.

For an instant we just fixed our eyes on one another. Then she just smiled. She had a very round tan little face with chubby cheeks. Her sun-streaked blonde hair was pulled into two little pigtails high on each side of her face. Her smile was broad and big, and her eyes squinted as her smile took over her little face … and then it hit me: I knew this little girl.

She was me!

Waves of emotion took hold of me as I stood there, immobilized, staring at her. Smiling back at me in her big, beautiful bed in her make-believe world. I don't think she knew who was smiling at her.

An overwhelming feeling of love for that cute little girl, as well as sorrow and sadness, took hold of me. I starting crying uncontrollably. She did not know what I would do to her in the future. She just sat there, in her sweetness and ignorance, in her make-believe world.

But I could see. I could see that she had an internal disease that was lying dormant in her DNA. It was horrifying and would eventually rear its ugly head and take her places that she never imagined she would go. But as I stood there crying, I knew. I could not stop the disease. It was a silent killer. There was no way to stop it or prevent it from metastasizing and spreading its destruction into every part of her life. Death lurking beneath her cute little chubby face, the sins of greed, rebellion, pride, self-sufficiency, all growing in her little heart like seeds just waiting for the time to bud and bring forth their ugly crop of destruction, producing a harvest of even more and more sin and death. For "whatever a man sows … he reaps" (Galatians 6:7).

Standing there in my sadness for what I knew she would do, for all the sadness and sorrow she would cause to herself, her parents and others along the way, I felt absolutely helpless and hopeless to help her. I wanted to rush to her, pick her up from her make-believe world and take her away to somewhere safe, somewhere I could protect her from the future I knew she would create for herself. But I knew I couldn't, so I just cried and prayed.

But then it happened. Someone from above.

A voice in the light said to me, "Don't be afraid, Thea. Before the foundation of the world I have set my love on her. Yes, she is still sick with sin and she can do nothing about her condition. Death is in her DNA. It has affected every part of her. Sin runs through her veins and it will ruin her life. She is young and it has not yet begun to bloom, but it will.

"But I am greater than her sin. I will come with healing in my wings. Awake, you sleeper, and rise from the dead and Christ will shine on you. For by grace have you been saved through faith and that not of yourselves—it is the gift of God. For we are His workmanship created in Christ Jesus for good works which God prepared beforehand that we should walk in them.

"But now, in Christ Jesus, you who were formerly far off have been brought near by the blood of Christ. For He Himself is our peace. For He came and preached peace to you who were far away and peace to you who were near for through Him we both have our access in one Spirit to the Father."

I was quieted.

Her smile—my smile—drew me to the bed. I slowly sat on the side of the bed with her. She crawled over to me and snuggled into my lap and I held her. I told her that I loved her and I was sorry for what I would do to her in the future but that we were not alone. Jesus was with her ... with me. That our sin would cause great harm but that the blood of Jesus our Savior was the purifier that could not be stopped. He was greater than our sin. He would come for us ... He has come for us.

In Christ we are free and Holy and well and at peace. We have a beautiful home awaiting us one day. A home where there is no sickness, no sin, no sorrow, no death, only joy in the presence of our Father and our Savior, Jesus Christ.

She just looked up at me with her big brown eyes and chubby face and smiled. She did not understand. She started playing with her teddy bear and started humming again.

I recognized the song. I sang it with her this time:

"God Will Take Care of You"
Civilla D. Martin

God will take care of you,
Through every day, o'er all the way;
He will take care of you,
God will take care of you.

22
Brown Crusty Bulbs and Blooming Beauty

PULLING MY 2-YEAR-OLD boy in his red wagon, I finally turned the corner into the long pine straw driveway of my parents' home. My son is my parent's ninth grandchild and the only one who has ever lived near them. We recently moved back here from Denver, Colorado, and rented a house only minutes from my old homestead in Beach Haven, Florida. I love it, and so does my little boy. Every day he begs to go see "Kapater" and "Mama Jo," the names of endearment given to them by their first grandchild many years ago.

Kapater, my father, recently retired and is thoroughly enjoying his newfound freedom. My mother, Mama Jo, never worked outside our home, but she is also enjoying my daddy's new lifestyle. They have done a little traveling, some fishing together, and enjoyed more time spent helping at the church in assorted ministries. But one of their favorite hobbies is working in their yard … and it shows! They both have green thumbs, and their yard is the prettiest on the block!

Finally reaching the end of the driveway, my anxious

2-year-old ran full speed to the screen door leading to the dining room, straight into the arms of the eagerly waiting Mama Jo and Kapater. They are thoroughly enjoying having a grandchild around for more than a short visit!

The room was filled with the aroma of freshly brewed coffee and cinnamon-raisin cookies. After a few hugs and kisses and two big cookies for each little hand, my son tagged along after his Kapater to go and "do chores." My father affectionately referred to my son as his "podnah," which is Southern for "partner," and that he was! The little 2-year-old was Kapater's "shadow" whenever they were together.

I settled down at the dining room table with my mother and sipped the steaming hot coffee, nibbled on her delicious warm cookies and enjoyed the view from their large dining room window.

I could see there were BIG plans going on outside in the front yard between the white-haired grandfather and his bright-eyed little helper.

The big metal wheelbarrow was filled with assorted tools. A large bag of fertilizer hung over one of the edges of the wheelbarrow. I could see a trowel, a yardstick and a bucket of something, probably bulbs.

It was early spring and my daddy planted at least 100 caladium bulbs in his flower beds each year! Everyone enjoyed the beautiful colorful leaves until the first frost. Then he would carefully dig them up and store them in a clean, dark place, only to replant them again in the springtime. One of the really neat things about bulbs is that they multiply each season! Beauty multiplying more beauty for all to enjoy!

Sipping my coffee, I watched my sweet white-haired father kneeling down next to the flower bed, digging a hole with his trowel. Six inches apart, then 6 inches deep, then add a little fertilizer and bone meal, then let the squirrely little 2-year-old drop the hard, crusty caladium bulb down into the hole, and then watch his little hands fill it up with dirt. "What a big boy he was to help him, yes sir-ree!" He was my father's little pod-nah! It was a sweet sight for the young mother!

Working within the two-minute attention span of any 2-year-old, my son would forget the planting and be running around the front yard looking for lizards or bugs or big slimy earth worms in the dirt of my parents' flower beds. The white-haired old man continued on his knees depositing in rich black soil his crusty, dry bulbs of future beauty! The work was hard each year but worth the wait! His beautiful caladiums had the largest leaves I have ever seen, with many assorted colorful patterns of green and red and white!

Sitting inside at the dining room table, my mother told me that "praying according to God's will" is a lot like planting bulbs. Planting your heart's desires in the rich soil of God's perfect, loving will! Just as many bulbs look the same on the outside, they are all different on the inside and only the Creator knows the beauty inside because He made it. You can't plant an acorn and get an apple tree. Nature is always true to itself and what is inside the seed will come out in due time. So be careful what you plant! Her words of wisdom.

My mother loved God's Word and spent countless hours there in intimacy with her Lord. She advised me many times that spending time in the Bible lets you see who God is and what is His will. That time with Him will allow you to grow in knowledge of His ways so you can have wisdom about what to pray for; otherwise, your prayers can be religious-sounding, pious whining from an impatient little child! Our prayers should reflect what the God of the Bible says is right and good and pleasing to Him. Many are not very thoughtful in how they pray. Most often we are just like my 2-year-old with the same attention span (short), with one speed (hurry up) and one desire (I want it now!)

So how should you pray? What should you pray for? What prayers can you plant and then trust God to bring them to fruition?

As you take time to seek God in solitude, you begin to think and grasp what truly are your deepest heart's desires. You must let those desires pass through the test of the Holy Spirit. You do that by taking your requests and then filtering them through the fruit of the Holy Spirit, which is love, joy, peace, patience, kindness, goodness, faithfulness, gentleness and self-control. We can spend a lifetime searching the inner treasures of these words of His grace and never come to the end of their beauty.

"But the fruit of the Spirit (the result of His Presence within us) is love (unselfish concern for others), joy (a settled contentment in God's will), peace (inner), patience (not just the ability to wait but how you act while you wait), kindness, goodness, faithfulness, gentleness and self-control. Against such things there is no law" (Galatians 5:22-23 Amplified Bible).

"Those who belong to Christ Jesus have crucified the flesh and its passions and desires. Since we live by the Spirit, let us keep in step with the Spirit" (Galatians 5:24-25).

I should ask myself when I pray, "Thea, is your desire full of the love of God? Do you love Him first? Do you love all others or are you still holding on to any unforgiveness or bitterness? Is your prayer selfish? Is it all about Thea?"

"Is your prayer of desire full of joy? Have I come to the place in my life that I am content in God alone and what He thinks is best? Am I looking for THIS answer to prayer to give me joy?"

"Is my desire full of peace to all? In making this request, will my inner attitude be one of a peacemaker?"

"Is my request full of patience? Am I willing to make the request and then be patient as God works whatever He thinks is best? Will I wait expectantly for the good always promised to His children, even if I must wait years or as long as He takes, even if the answer comes after I am gone from this earth?"

On and on she would go through the scriptures, challenging my inner thoughts of prayer and how I viewed the God of the Bible and how He works and what He wanted for His glory.

Meditations on the fruit of the Holy Spirit help us to see our own shallowness and selfishness and then gives Him time to work tenderly on our inner self, convicting, cleansing and then restoring our soul so we can truly want what He wants, whatever that might be. Prayers that pass through the washing of the Holy Spirit are then finally ready to be received into our hearts as His will for us, started in heaven then placed in our heart by God, for us to then ask to be given to us, for our good and His glory. Once we know them, then we plant them in order to LET GO of them completely!

Just as my daddy planted those hard, crusty brown bulbs and then was content to wait for the beauty that would eventually come forth, so too, must we pray.

My daddy knew that there was a miracle going on 6 inches deep in the dark, rich Beach Haven soil of that flowerbed. He waited. He watered. He watched expectantly for signs of growth. How foolish he would have been if he had dug up the bulbs every week to see if they were growing.

All he needed to do was weed, if needed, and make sure they had water … and just wait expectantly.

So too, after we plant our heart's desire in prayer, we must LET IT GO. But we may need to weed our hearts as we wait. If we see fear or worry or impatience sprout within us, we must confess it and receive God's cleansing. Sometimes we water with our tears of love and faith and trust in our God who knows what is best. And we wait in expectation for the beauty that will eventually bloom in God's timing!

My mother prayed all the time, but I knew that very early in the morning, long before her family woke, she would be seated on the end of the couch, with Bible and hymnal in hand, seeking to know the Lord and enjoy His presence before the sun ever rose in her little Beach Haven paradise.

This memory that lives in my head has been there more than 40 years. The little 2-year-old is now in his mid-40s, and the white-haired grandfather went to heaven years and years ago. The wise grandmother died living in a mind that Alzheimer's devoured, and then she joined her Beloved forever. And the young mother … well, she listened at the dining room table that day, but the seeds of truth took years before they germinated in her own soul.

Thea had to grow up.

Hurtful things helped me let go of selfish praying and finally made me receptive to the only Power that could change a soul: surrender at the cross of Christ! My attention span with God changed from the short span of a toddler to one who lived to seek His face. My speed changed from "hurry up, God" to lingering long in His presence, for He is enough. My desire changed from a childish "I want what I want, when I want it, cuz I'm the boss of me" to waiting silently before the Sovereign God of everything, praying, "Not my will, but Thine be done."

I wish I could tell Mama Jo how much she taught me. Her words of truth still linger in my head and help to guide me as I pray. My prayers have certainly changed over the years. I have enjoyed seeing many, many answered prayers! Bulbs grew up and blossomed, but others, planted from my heart, still lay dormant in the soil of God's love.

But I'm still waiting and looking expectantly!

Thank you, Lord! I see flowers blooming!

"Every day I will praise You, and I will praise Your Name forever. Great is the Lord, and greatly to be praised; and His greatness is unsearchable. One generation shall praise Your works to another and shall declare Your mighty acts. I will meditate on the glorious splendor of Your majesty and on Your wondrous works. Men shall speak of Your awesome acts, and I will declare Your greatness, they shall utter the memory of Your great goodness, and shall sing of Your righteousness" (Psalm 145:2-7).

23
The Spirit from Christmas Past

THERE IT WAS, right in the center of my parent's living room. Sitting on a small coffee table against the wall was a 4-foot Christmas tree.

As a child I remember going with my father to pick out our evergreen tree at the Christmas tree lot near our home. I can still remember walking behind him, smelling the evergreens and getting excited about decorating our tree when we got home. Daddy would always make sure the one he picked out was to my liking. It was fun to help him tie the tree on top of our old car and then watch him as he would set it up in our living room. Later that night or early the next day, I would help my mother and older sister decorate the tree while we sang Christmas carols.

I grew up when Christmas was mostly about the baby Jesus. Of course, I believed in Santa Claus, but my parents made sure that I always knew that we celebrated Christmas because we were celebrating the birth of Jesus our Savior. There were manger scenes set up in all the stores, schools had plays about baby Jesus and we sang Christmas carols in our school rooms.

But times were a-changing!

I witnessed something very peculiar in my parents' home that year. It seemed so out of place in the little modest home of Jo Burge, my mother.

My mother believed in living in simplicity. She was always very neat and orderly. She was also frugal and modest and did not give in to "flashiness" in any shape or form. But my daddy … now he was a different story! She would tease him and say he just loved "puttin' on the Ritz!" (It was years before I knew that was a song written in the late '20s, inspired by the Ritz Carlton Hotel, the place of the "fashionably" wealthy!)

I think my daddy might have been "puttin' on the Ritz" when they bought that Christmas tree. It was during the 1970s, and things were "a-changin'" for sure.

There it was, in all its 4 feet of aluminum glory! A small rotating color wheel was sitting on the floor, slowly spinning, reflecting its colors on the lifeless aluminum arms.

This Christmas was supposed to be a very special one! My older sister and her family were coming to spend the holidays here with us in Beach Haven. She hadn't spent Christmas with her family in many years. I'd been living in Pensacola for the last four years, and we were all excited to finally be together again! My mother had been busy baking all sorts of goodies and counting the hours until her oldest daughter and her husband would arrive with her three precious granddaughters.

Finally, my sister arrived and after all the hugs, kisses, laughing, talking and dragging suitcases inside, we finally worked our way into our parents' living room … and there it was: the 4-foot lifeless aluminum tree with its spinning colors of pink and blue lights!

One look from my sister and "NO, this will NOT do!" We needed a real Christmas tree and she was going to get one! But where can you get a real Christmas tree very late on Christmas Eve? It didn't matter; she had to try, so off she went!

Finally, after searching for anything open, she found one lot with a few scraggly trees still left. The lot manager, getting ready to leave, just said, "Take whatever you want and Merry Christmas!" With the straggly little tree tied to the top of their car, she rushed back home to mother and daddy's house to "de-aluminize" their Christmas décor!

With her three daughters and my little boy, we set out to do some home-spun decorating! Right away, my sister and I starting baking gingerbread cookies! Two of the kids starting stringing popcorn, and the other two strung bright-red cranberry garland. In between, our mother was helping us with paper chains and folded white paper snowflakes to cut out. The newly introduced cousins were laughing like they'd known each other for years! We all sang Christmas carols, and my sister and I enjoyed singing harmony with our mother like we used to when we washed and dried dishes with her.

The whole house was saturated with the aroma of evergreen branches, cinnamon, ginger and popcorn! Finally, our little scraggly evergreen was decorated by all the kids. We just stood back and enjoyed our masterpiece! It was truly magnificent! Yes, I thought I saw some tears welling up in mama' eyes!

Calling everyone into the dining room to begin our Christmas Eve tradition, my mother turned off all the lights. We were all crammed into the small room sitting in the dark. A single candle was lit in the center of the table, sitting next to one of mama's delicious sour-cream coffee cakes. It was time to be serious and really think about why we have Christmas.

As per tradition, my mother brought out her Bible and read the passage in Luke about the birth of Christ. Then she prayed, and we all held hands and sang "Happy Birthday" to Jesus! Later, as we were all enjoying eggnog and coffee cake, she read "The Night Before Christmas." We ended the night singing more carols!

Everyone was tired from the trip and all the grandchildren were finally getting sleepy. They made pallets in the floor of one of the bedrooms and decided to all sleep together! Of course, there was WAY too much giggling going on before the cousins finally fell asleep.

The next day was Christmas and what a wonderful time it was. Opening presents from under our rescued "real" Christmas tree and the kids still talking about how much fun they had! At lunch we devoured a magnificent Christmas meal with our mother's delicious turkey and dressing with all the trimmings!

Later that day, after a nap, we drove around the corner to the house of my mother's twin brother and his wife, affectionately known as "Onkie" and "Ankie." Ankie made the best homemade candy ever and Onkie was a concert pianist. We enjoyed our Onkie's Christmas repertoire, then ended our visit by singing carols around his baby grand piano.

It was one of the best Christmases I ever experienced! Full of love for family, the simple pleasure of decorating our homespun Christmas tree and singing songs of praise for the Christ of Christmas. But in my reminiscing about this Christmas, there is also a sadness in my memory. It was the last Christmas with our daddy. My father died just four months later. He'd been bragging at Christmas that the doctor told him he had the heart of a 16-year-old! What did he know? A heart attack took my daddy at age 66, looking strong and healthy, the ideal specimen of a senior citizen! One Sunday he was serving communion in church, the next Sunday he was in heaven. You never know when you'll spend the last Christmas with someone you love.

I love Christmas and all the wonderful memories I hold in my heart involving that special holiday. But certainly, Christmas is NOT all about family! My daddy loved his family dearly and in the months following, he often spoke of that sweet time he enjoyed with his family and grandchildren. But my daddy's spirit was prepared to die. He lived each day with that peace. But would he have chosen to go so early? I don't think so, but I know where he is, and I look forward to the day I will see him again and my mother and many who have gone ahead. I am grateful that my parents taught me how to love, the importance of family and friends, of enjoying the beauty of simple pleasures with a grateful heart, but most of all, their example of faith in the Lord.

I close this happy holiday memory with an entry from Mama Jo's journal:

"Heavenly Father, my prayer is a simple one, whatever is best for me to do, in sickness, in health; I desire what brings the most glory to you! I do not know what the coming year holds, but one thing I know; I know the One who holds us in His hands! Amen."

24
Little Green Sprout in a Concrete Crack

STANDING AT MY kitchen sink, I felt the weight of my 2-year-old sitting on my foot and her chubby arms clutching my legs, her voice whimpering, "My mama, my mama."

I held my 3-month-old infant like a football next to my side, balancing her on my right arm, while using my left hand to gather ingredients from the refrigerator and begin dinner.

My older son sat at the kitchen table with homework spread everywhere, whining about how long it's taking him to write his spelling words and why he has to do so much homework in the first place.

Everyone was tugging at me, pulling me, stretching me, needing me, and inwardly I screamed. Then softly I told my son to stop his complaining and get busy. Those spelling words aren't going anywhere and the sooner he finishes them, the sooner he can go outside and play.

My inward scream faded in my head as I once again looked at the faces of the three children I love so much. They are so precious to me. "O God, help me."

I was a young mother in a very hard place. My marriage was headed for disaster. I felt like I was free-falling from an airplane and I had no parachute! Daily, I screamed inside with fear and panic and deep sorrow, but at the same time, I rocked my babies, sang old hymns and read nursery rhymes and asked myself, "Am I doing enough to hide it all from my precious ones? I so want their little world safe and secure and happy."

But that day I tasted the emptiness of the cup I so desperately tried to fill up. I felt a crack in my make-believe world that I tried so hard to control. "God, help me, I can't lose what I want so much!" Being a wife and a mother was all I ever wanted and I was seeing it slip through my fingers like the slippery soap I felt as I washed the dishes in the sink.

I often think about that day in my kitchen. It was the beginning of my journey out of my own denial — the inward scream of my heart seeking serenity and peace.

It was years before I actually turned the corner and started traveling down the road of peace to seek the face of God each morning in His Holy Word. But one day, the full crack came and shattered the hard cocoon of my make-believe world.

I was a young Christian woman, and I was really trying to be good. I took my kids to church each week. I tried to have a quiet time every day, to read a verse in the Bible and say my prayers. I even used a short devotional for women to get a daily dose of some spiritual thought to give me a little encouragement. But in reality, it was more like the pep talk my son's football coach gave to the team on Saturday mornings at the ball park: "You can do it. You have what it takes. You're strong! You worked hard. You deserve to win. Winners never quit!" It was all about me, helping me, and I had done that for years and it wasn't working.

I was getting tired of the pep talks and weary of this game called life in my world—or should I say, in my multiple worlds! Who was I? I didn't even know, and the only thing I did know was that I was sad, scared, filled with fear and tired … very, very tired.

And all of this was good for me, very good for me. Even though I felt terrible, it was good for me.

"It was good that I was afflicted, for it taught me to heed my ways" *(Psalm 119:71).*

My heart was "in process," in construction mode. I felt so out of control—so in desperation, I tried to grab hold and control everyone and everything around me.

Everything was under control, of course, but under the control of the loving hand of the Sovereign God who works all things together for His purposes and for the good of His children. I knew I was one of His children. That is the one thing I did know for sure. Nothing else really made sense, but I knew THAT was truth and so I held on to it!

Growing up in a Christian home, going to church my entire life, millions of seeds of truth had been deposited into my head. My parents, my Sunday school and youth group leaders, Bible school and flannel graft stories, missionaries and preachers, they had all done their part sowing seeds into me that had been lying dormant for years!

Then one day, 10 years earlier, in a small basement apartment in Denver, Colorado, a seed fell from my head to my heart and a new life was born. Life from above! The truth about who Jesus was and what He accomplished on the cross gave birth to a new me! But the new me was still a "baby me," and there was much to do to help me grow up.

Disillusioned dreams and princess pride had coated my heart with the concrete illusion of self-control. There was much work to be done, and I whined profusely as all children, who must sit down and do homework when all they really want is to throw away the book and go outside and play!

Thank the Lord; He is too wise to give into our constant whining. He always does what is best for us and to bring Himself glory! It's really all about Him anyway, but I hadn't learned that lesson yet!

As the seed of truth took root within my heart, cracks began to happen … everywhere! Desperately I tried to hold it all together, but the living seed can't be stopped! The life force within that seed of truth grew and it continued to crack through the concrete illusion—boulders flew off in every direction!

My little world was crumbling and as hard as I tried, I couldn't keep it all together. I tried to keep my babies close to me in my make-believe world. After all, they were the ones I lived for. Isn't that what all good mothers do, live for their children? No, but I hadn't learned that lesson either.

Bulldozers came and turned everything upside down. Large boulders had to go and there was no telling God, "No, You can't have that" and "Not this, God, this is mine." It was all His anyway, but I hadn't learned that lesson either. I was trying so hard to put all the concrete pieces back together again!

Isn't God supposed to help me hold everything together? And you're right, I hadn't learned that lesson either. Only He could hold it all together and that was to be enough for His child.

The little girl who spent her childhood playing pretend princess was now feeling like Humpty Dumpty who had fallen off the wall, finally realizing she could not put it all together again. It was scary and lonely!

Miles away from the young mother in the kitchen, there was another mother on her knees, taking her sick daughter to the Healer.

The "knee-mother" would have done anything to help her daughter; she loved her. But the knee-mother was a wise woman who knew much more than the pretend princess.

The knee-mother knew where to go. She didn't barge into the kitchen of her sick daughter. She didn't try to take control of the mess she was in. She just quietly went to the only place she knew of to fix a sick soul: at the feet of Jesus. She prayed, watered her prayer with her tears, and left her little sick daughter there.

"Wherever He came, in villages, cities or countryside, they laid the sick in the marketplaces and begged Him that they might touch the hem of His garment" (Mark 6:56a).

And for THAT touch, the knee-mother prayed.

Then one day, years later, the young Christian mother, the one who used to live in the kitchen with her three children in her make-believe world, THAT mother stopped living there. The living seed of faith that had sprouted long before grew and broke through the hard concrete of her heart, forced its way up through the cracks and the flying boulders, and then began to grow something beautiful in the broken and fertile soil of the not-so-young mother's heart!

"Oh, God, thank you. My heart is now filled with the JOY of the Lord. How can this be?"

I remember now … I had finally learned this lesson. Prayer, God's Word and surrender, that's the way of peace.

The knee-mother prayed and left her sick little daughter in the marketplace at the feet of Jesus, the Healer.

"And as many as touched Him, He made well" (Mark 6:56b).

He touched the not-so-young mother just as He had touched the knee-mother years before. He made them whole! He brought streams in the desert, light in the darkness, beauty out of ashes and joy out of sadness.

Would I want anything to be different? No, it was good for me that I was afflicted for it taught me to heed my way and gave birth to the greatest pleasure my heart could possibly ever know, joy in God alone!

"You will show me the path of life; in Your presence is fullness of joy; in Your right hand there are pleasures forevermore" (Psalm 16:11).

25
Morning Glory Brigade

LITTLE HANDS TUGGED at my apron strings. "Please, mommy, can we go to JoJo's? Can we pick her some flowers?"

And so began the almost daily ritual of "the walk."

Mama Jo and Kapater were my children's grandparents who lived just a quarter of a mile from us. It was a daily expectation to go to JoJo's house. It didn't matter if it was summer or winter; they wanted to go. We could always find some magical expression of God's creation along the path to their grandparents' house. It was always an adventure!

So began the routine of tying little tennis shoes, washing smudges off faces and then the kids running out to board their bikes!

Even though it was only a few blocks away, it could take hours to get there, as we never went in a straight path. The road took several turns, which only made them want to go round and round in circles along the way. We passed the time singing songs: "Three Blind Mice," "Row, Row, Row Your Boat," "Jesus Loves Me"! Nursery rhymes and Sunday school songs filled the air of our winding path to JoJo's house.

We stopped along the way to see what "neat stuff" we

would find, such as old bird nests that had fallen from the big oak tree and empty locust shells. Of course, that would always bring about deep questions such as, "How did the locust know it was time to leave his shell?" and "Did it hurt when he took off his shell?" There were kudzu vines growing everywhere, gracefully falling over the tall pine braches like icicles on Christmas trees.

But the most magical moment was the explosion of the morning glories!

Little feet peddled hard around the sharp bend in the path and then there they were like purple paint flung across the sky! They were everywhere, from the tallest pine tree to each tiny blade of grass, like fingers gently holding and caressing everything they touched. A blanket of glorious purple covered the horizon just waiting for little hands to fall into their embrace.

Bikes were tossed to the ground as the children ran toward the morning glories. They began the serious business of finding just the right ones to pick for JoJo. Their tiny little fingers could only hold so many and they had to be just right for their grandmother!

I would sit along the dusty roadside and just watch. They busied themselves in their task, lost in the ocean of purple until they had picked just the right ones. With the perfect bouquet in hand, we continued our journey with purple treasures grasped by tiny little fingers.

They peddled their little bikes hard and excitedly entered her long driveway. Lined with tall Florida pines and a pine straw path, we heard whistling and smelled coffee brewing, a sure sign that JoJo was home!

The screen door was jerked open with a frenzy and little sweaty hands and crushed morning glories were thrust toward JoJo with big smiles: "Look what we brought you, JoJo!" Oh, the thrill and excitement she showed for the pitifully bruised purple flowers! "Why, these are the most beautiful flowers I've ever seen" and "What lovely children you are to bring them to me!" She would carefully place them in an empty jelly jar and set them right next to her placemat at the dining room table. She said that way she could look at them ALL day long! With that, a kiss on the forehead and a fingertip to the nose, she would present them with a Popsicle and then send them off to play outside while mom and JoJo shared a cup of coffee.

It's a memory from long ago ... just an ordinary day with an ordinary woman, her sweet little children and their grandmother. Each time I see the color purple, I think of magical morning glories and treasured moments of long walks and remember the "feel" of love.

A glorious morning from an ordinary day, but a treasure to me—my parents, my children and God's beautiful purple morning glories experienced along a winding pavement path in Beach Haven many, many years ago.

"This is the day the Lord has made; we will rejoice and be glad in it" *(Psalm 118:24).*

26
Secret Moments

THE NIGHT WAS calm and still. Darkness filled the rooms as I stumbled down the hallway to the kitchen for a glass of water.

Standing at my kitchen sink, I stared out into the darkness and saw the light of the moon casting a warm and comforting glow over our backyard. I stood there a moment, alone in my silent thoughts, then made my way back to bed.

As I walked down the dark hallway, I stopped at the bedroom of my little one.

There she was, sound asleep, a few toys left out on the floor, a book opened at the end of the bed. The room was dark, but the faint glow of the moon's light was peeking through the window shades.

I saw her small, angelic face resting on her crumpled pillow. I sat down next to her on the bed and just watched her. Her sweet little mouth, slightly open, breathing silently. Her pudgy hands clasping her covers tightly up under her chin. So sweet … so relaxed … so innocent. What a beautiful child God had given me. Oh how I loved this child of mine. At times, my heart wanted to burst because the love I felt was so intense.

I just sat there and stared at her. With my hand, I stroked her hair; my eyes traced every part of her face. Her head, so perfectly round, those soft little ears, her cute button nose and then those lips ... so sweet ... I gently dropped a kiss on her brow.

She just lay there, oblivious to her mother's presence with her.

Thoughts wandered through my mind. What does life hold for my little one? Right then it was full of bicycles and sleepovers, homework and science fair projects and sometimes restrictions for mess-ups so she could learn right from wrong.

Another rush of love surged within my heart and then at the same time, pain mingled with fear. Oh, I wished I could guarantee her life would always be easy and free of worry or pain. I wished I could make sure her life was full of happiness and security, joy and peace, but I knew that could not be.

I heard the sound of a car driving down the street outside. In a few moments, its headlights filled her room like the morning sunshine but she didn't move a muscle and then darkness came again.

I sat beside her in the stillness of the night ... five minutes, then 10, then half an hour. "I love you, I pray for you. I sing songs to the Lord for you."

"God Will Take Care of You"
Civilla D. Martin

Be not be dismayed, whate'er betide,
God will take care of you!
Beneath His wings of love abide, God will take care of you!
God will take care of you!
Thru every day, o'er all the way; He will take care of you;
God will take care of you!

I prayed for God's protection for her. I prayed for God's wisdom for her. I prayed that He would come to her and make Himself known to her and fill her heart with His love. I prayed that He would fulfill His purpose for her life, my sweet little one. As I continued sitting there, staring at her, loving her, once again I stroked her hair away from her brow. She began to stir and roll over.

I looked up at the clock and I couldn't believe I had been sitting there for over an hour, alone in the dark with her. Secret moments … just my sweet little one and me and God.

Then I heard, "Get up, Thea, get back to bed. You need some rest. It's almost dawn and there's a busy day awaiting you."

Slowly I got up and moved down the hallway and back into my own bed.

My soft pillow felt good under my head. I pulled the comforter up under my chin and sang to myself.

"Thea, 'God will take care of you. Thru every day, o'er all the way; He will take care of you; God will take care of you!'"

"The Lord your God in your midst, The Mighty One, will save; He will rejoice over you with gladness, He will quiet you with His love, He will rejoice over you with singing" (Zephaniah 3:17).

"And He took them up in His arms, laid His hands on them and blessed them" (Mark 10:16).

"For He shall give His angels charge over you, to keep you in all your ways" (Psalm 91:11).

27
Whispers in the Night
(My Journey into Joy)

MUFFLED SOUNDS, WHEELS turning, pain and darkness … deep, overpowering darkness. Then, faintly, a small light flickered and then a voice. A strong but soothing voice within: "Where there is darkness, let me sow light."

Pain … "Oh, my God, this hurts!" My eyes burned from the bright lights above; I strained to see more. I tried to swallow but choked instead. I coughed and the intense pain brought me to reality. I remember now. I had just had surgery and I was in the recovery room. Just one week before, I had gone to my doctor's appointment only to hear his rebuke again that my pap tests had come back with precancerous cells. This was my third test with the same results, and his warning to me was that I needed to have a hysterectomy right away. Once again, I began my list of why I couldn't do it right at this time. Yes, I would have the surgery soon, but too many were depending on me right now. There was no way to stop and have immediate surgery. He told me sternly that he had heard my excuses before and today he was calling the hospital and scheduling me for surgery that week. He'd been my doctor for years, and I trusted him, so I went along with his plan. My surgery took place a few days later, and now there I was in the recovery room in excruciating pain.

But something else had just happened to me and I certainly didn't understand it.

Why, in the stillness of my mind, coming out of surgery, did I hear those clear, soft words so plainly? And where did they come from? What did it mean?

For the next several years, God took me down a path of discovery to show me what He meant by His whispers in the night.

Of course, He started long before the whispers, as it was His love that placed me in a condition that allowed me to finally begin to hear. Ironically, I was strapped down to a gurney! I wasn't going anywhere, and I wasn't doing anything for anyone. I was certainly not too busy there! Perhaps, finally tied down, I would shut up and learn to listen!

How naïve to think that God wants us always well and happy, for so often that is where we think we are self-sufficient and self-reliant and feel very self-satisfied without Him. It is most often in our weakness and our helplessness that we finally begin to experience His tender love and mercy as we let go of self and listen for His words that bring peace and love and healing.

I grew up in a family that believed in hard work and determination! The Burges were NOT quitters! It was drilled into me that quitters never win! And I wanted to win! But somewhere in my journey through life, that not-quitting philosophy became my mantra for self-exalting pride. I believed there was nothing I couldn't handle. Hard work and determination could get you anything! That mind-set is what put me deeper into my darkness. There is so much in life we have absolutely NO control over, and all the hard work and determination can NEVER make it change! The brick wall is there. It's hard and insurmountable and it hurts each time we try to plow through it with our headstrong determination.

Oh, the precious grace and mercy of God with his refining ministry of pain.

Alone in the darkness, sitting against my brick wall, I got tired. Year after year, trying to figure out a way to go through the brick wall left me puzzled about myself and God. After years of self-determination, I found myself emotionally battered and bruised. There were wounds in my soul, crusted over, only seconds away from oozing again their festered message that reminded me, "Thea, you are a failure. You can't get through the wall!"

But I didn't want to be a failure. I didn't want to be a quitter. "God, please help me. I'm dying here, next to the brick wall gasping for air." I slowly began to humble myself and in some slight way accepted my helplessness and the sickness of this body of mine. And now, here I was coming out from surgery. My whole life hurt and none of it made sense!

My recuperation from my hysterectomy turned into a long ordeal. There were complications after surgery, and I was confined to bedrest.

I was bored … you can only watch so much TV! As an adult, I had not been much of a reader. I'm the artsy/creative type and any free time I have, I use it painting or sewing or cooking or doing crafts. Reading … not so much! But maybe, now that I was confined, I might give reading a try.

I walked slowly down the hallway to the bookshelf and grabbed a real skinny book. As I pulled it off the shelf, I realized it was one my mother gave to me years before. Leafing through the yellowing pages, I laughed and wondered how long it had been sitting on my bookshelf.

I thought, "Oh well, it's short, so I think I'll start with this one."

The little book was about praise, and much of it was taken from the book of Philippians, which was written by Paul, who happened to be in prison when he wrote the book. That should be interesting! I could identify with a prisoner. But surprisingly enough, it was all about joy, something I knew little about.

I had firsthand knowledge about denial, fear, worry, loneliness and pain, but deep joy: definitely not one of my close companions. So I read on …

Reading through the little book, my eyes stopped on a verse of scripture. I read the words over and over again.

"Don't worry about anything but pray and ask God for everything you need, always giving thanks. And the peace of God which surpasses understanding will keep your hearts and minds safe in Christ Jesus" (Philippians 4:6-7).

Staring at those words, I muttered under my breath, "God, this is crazy!"

And so began my dialogue with God that changed the course of my life:

"God, how can You say 'don't worry'? Do You see my life? And even if You're not watching me, certainly You can hear my voice as I pray to You night and day, telling You what's going on and begging You to do something ... anything! But nothing ever changes, and I am dying inside more and more each day and now I'm stuck in this bed, reading a yellowed book of my mother's, telling me not to worry! Are You kidding me, God? Do You think I enjoy living in a head that worries all the time?"

Almost throwing the book aside in irritation, I couldn't stop myself from staring at those words of scripture.

Like a neon sign they began to illuminate my thoughts: "Don't worry ... BE thankful."

In curiosity, I grabbed my Bible and looked into my concordance to find the words "thankful" and "thankfulness."

Wow, it was everywhere: Be thankful for ALL things, IN all things, THROUGH all things. Be thankful as a sacrifice to God and then in James, we are to count our problems as joy instead?

I thought, "This is crazy, God! None of the things that consume me in fear and worry are good. How can I thank You for something I am not thankful for?"

Reading through the rest of Philippians 4, I thought I saw an answer. Verse 13 says, "I can do all things through Him who strengthens me." "OK, God, I cannot do this, but You can, so here we go."

I grabbed a long yellow legal pad and began my list of woes. None of them were good; all of them were hurting me, crushing the life out of me.

Before long, my yellow notepad was filled with problems, all of which I had spent a lifetime trying to change and I had failed to make a difference in.

Now I began to do what I had never done before, to thank

God for my problems. I had always tried to look for the best and be grateful for all the blessings God had given me, but this was new territory for me and it didn't make sense at all. But I saw it written down in the Bible, right in front of my eyes, in black and white, and so I began.

"God, I thank you for problem #1, problem #2, problem #3, and #4 …" and down, down, down I went through my list of woes. It wasn't too long down the list that I found myself crying uncontrollably. Sobs of guilt of seeing my own blame of others, of my pride of life thinking life was all about me and even my anger at God for not giving me what I thought I deserved. Then abruptly my tears changed and I found myself feeling lighter and more peaceful, and my tears were tears of joy! The kind of tears I had not felt since I was first converted at age 21. It was wonderful. This must be what my mother had been trying to tell me for years but I wasn't ready to hear her or obey the Word of God when I didn't understand it.

My sickroom seemed to glow with light and the presence and peace of God appeared like a warm blanket I was wrapped up in, and I didn't want it to stop. I guess this is what that verse meant … the peace that passes understanding. God's peace that will keep my heart and mind safe IN Christ.

All of a sudden, life got simple again. I just quit! I wasn't strong or self-sufficient or self-reliant or self-satisfied; I was weak and needy and empty and enormously filled with JOY!

Something had happened TO me. I think it was what happened to Paul: "Not that I am speaking of being in need, for I have learned in whatever situation I am to be content. I know how to be brought low and how to abound. In any and every circumstance, I have learned the SECRET of facing plenty and hunger, abundance and need. I can do all things through HIM who strengthens me. And my God will supply every need of yours according to His riches in glory IN Christ Jesus. To our God and Father be glory forever and ever amen" (Philippians 4:11-13, 19-20).

For years I treated God like a drive-through pharmacy. He wanted me to learn that only He is God and will not be treated lightly with such disrespect. By experience I needed to learn that He alone is God and He was not there to meet my every whim. He will humble us so we can taste our emptiness and feel the need of the only power that can change the human heart … HIS! Brick walls are necessary in the journey, and they are numerous. It's amazing and exhilarating to see how joyful we can be as we taste how small we really are and focus on the greatness of our God. HE, not His gifts, IS the never-ending pleasure!

It's all about HIM! All I need to do is trust in His Word and keep on praising Him all the way home!

"YOU make known to me the path of life; in YOUR presence there is fullness of JOY; at YOUR right hand there are pleasures forevermore" (Psalm 16:11).

28
Showers of Blessings

THE COLD TILE stretched out before me. Darkness surrounded me like a garment. Warm water streamed down my head; curled up in a little ball, I lay weeping. Shedding waves of tears with groans too deep for words, I trembled in my loneliness.

Sitting alone on the tile floor in my shower in the dark, I cried … again.

I don't know how many nights I spent this way, but it became my place of refuge.

My children were asleep. The house was quiet. I heard a clock ticking in my bedroom: 10 o'clock … 11 o'clock … 12 o'clock, then 1 o'clock … 2 o'clock … alone again.

No more pacing the floor, no more peeking through the window blinds at the sound of each passing car, no more anger or fear or worry… just cold tile, in the dark, with warm water beating down my back.

Slowly I began to sing and rock myself.

"Turn Your Eyes Upon Jesus"
Helen H. Lemmel

Turn your eyes upon Jesus. Look full in His wonderful face

and the things of earth will grow strangely dim in the light of
His glory and grace.

I don't remember when it began, when my heart began to
crack.

The years of "no tears" began to seep with living water …
but the tears came, and I broke.

Emotional pain makes you hard. Sometimes the rejected
heart can only survive life by pulling down thick walls to protect the festering wounds. Living the masked life is the only
way you can function and continue through the duties of daily
life. Taking care of the kids, cooking meals, cleaning the house,
running errands, trips to the ball park and yes, even the duties
of being married—you just have to get on with life. Just keep on
going. Smile. Keep your chin up. Try to stay positive and make
the best of the situation.

But somewhere in all my phoniness, God touched the deepest recesses of my heart and brought tears to me as a gift.

I can't tell you how many, many nights I spent crying alone
in the shower, but it was redemptive. Rocking back and forth
and singing old hymns to myself was comforting. Instinctively
I felt like I was a chubby-faced little girl, dirty from playing in
the mud, and my mother was washing me, singing to me …
loving me … except now I knew it was the Lord.

I was not alone. He cared. He saw. I was safe there; no need
for a mask in the shower. Realness took hold of me. I broke.
Tears welled up and they burst forth and shattered the dam. At
first, all that rose from my soul was ugliness, deep and hidden
anger and bitterness and blame. Like a festering wound, my

sins poured out. I had covered it for so long, trying to make the best of my life. But God knew the real me, and I needed to see myself. I needed to quit blaming others and see me the way God saw me: dirty, angry, bitter, self-righteous, wounded, needy, weak, afraid but unconditionally loved and cherished.

I prayed, "O, God, I'm sorry, I repent, here … now, in this dark bathroom with warm water running over my body. Rocking, shaking, I cry … I have sinned against You, O God; cleanse my heart of this anger and bitterness. Heal me, God. I am desperate. I don't want to live like this anymore … I can't live like this. I need You, Lord."

With my sinful bleeding heart exposed, I saw there what I had never seen before: idols.

I was a Christian woman looking for love, wanting and needing a man to fill up the deep void within my soul. I thought at first my husband would do that but after years of a very painful marriage, I began looking to my children. Oh how I loved my little ones. They were my life, my joy, my heart, my all and yet, I still could feel an emptiness and sense a deep whisper that man is never enough to fill a heart with love and peace and joy. I faced the vacuum in my heart that could only be filled with God alone.

Sitting alone in my shower, rocking and singing, streams of living water bathed my empty soul.

The tears had washed the eyes of my soul so I could clearly see. O thank you, Father, it's Jesus … Jesus is who I need, who I have always needed and will always need! The Only Begotten of the Father, full of grace and truth!

I prayed: "My soul weeps because of grief. Strengthen me

according to Thy Word. (Psalm 119:28) But the Lord has helped me. The Lord is my strength and song. He has become my salvation. The sound of joyful shouting and salvation is in the tents of the righteous. The right hand of the Lord is exalted; the right hand of the Lord does valiantly. I shall not die, but live and tell of the works of the Lord. The Lord has disciplined me severely but He has not given me over to death. Open to me the gates of righteousness. I shall enter through them; I shall give thanks to the Lord. This is the gate of the Lord. The righteous will enter through it. I shall give thanks to Thee. For thou hast answered me, and Thou hast become my salvation" (Psalm 118:14–21).

Like my mother washing her dirty little girl, the presence of the Lord washed my soul in those dark and warm showers so many, many years ago.

"This poor man cried out, and the Lord heard him. And saved him out of all his troubles" (Psalm 34:6).

Someone asked me recently if I ever took trips back to the dark shower. My answer was, "Yes, but not so often anymore."

I found out that when the Lord saves you out of all your troubles, that doesn't mean He removes any of them, except from our own hands. Getting out of the shower so long ago didn't mean I was walking into a life without the same problems, I was just not holding them anymore. His Presence there with me in the dark shower helped me to surrender. In weariness, my twisted fingers let go of all that I was holding so close. I could not carry it anymore. I am weak, He is strong. I was trying to control people and situations, but He WAS and IS always in control. I was fearful and weary, but He assured me that He would carry me through whatever I must go through. I felt alone and unloved, but that was a lie. I am eternally loved and kept by Almighty God. The absence of problems did not come to me, but the Person of Peace came in the midst of my darkness and deep inner JOY began to slowly trickle through my veins.

So, do I take the trip to the shower anymore? Not much. Only when I focus on "me" too long and forget Who is really in charge. "I have learned to be content in whatever state I am" (Philippians 4:11).

My now pastor husband often reminds me that all of God's children are always safe in the palm of His hand. At times, He opens His fingers and lets difficulties touch our lives, but the end is always for our good and His glory, even though we may not understand it at the time. Romans 8:28 promises us that "God causes ALL things to work together for good to those who are the called according to HIS purpose."

Walking in gratitude and thanksgiving helps keep me focused and free. Praising Him for all things, through all things and for all things helps me keep my eyes on Jesus, so that the things of life really do grow strangely dim in the light of His glory and grace.

Psalm 22:3 tells us that "He inhabits the praise of his people." He makes His presence sweet to us as we focus on Him, praise Him and remember His promises to us.

I often tell young mothers, busy with young children and the whirlwind of duties during that season of their life, to run to the shower at night. When your children are all tucked in and asleep, the dishwasher is humming its last task for the night, run to Jesus. Thank Him for all things. Surrender all!

"Turn Your Eyes Upon Jesus"
Helen H. Lemmel

Turn your eyes upon Jesus. Look full in His wonderful face and the things of earth will grow strangely dim in the light of His glory and grace.

Even on a cold tile floor in a dark, warm shower in the middle of the night, run to the Lord.

"I love the Lord because He hears my voice and my supplications. Because He has inclined His ear to me, therefore I shall call upon Him as long as I live" (Psalm 116:1-2).

"For it is the God who commanded light to shine out of darkness, who has shone in our hearts, to give the light of the knowledge of the Glory of God in the face of Jesus Christ" (2 Corinthians 4:6).

"Come to Me, all you who are weary and heavy laden and I will give you rest. Take My yoke upon you and learn from Me, for I am gentle and lowly in heart and you will find rest for your souls. For My yoke is easy and My burden is light" (Matthew 11:28-30).

29
My Praying Tree

HURRIEDLY WALKING OUT the front door, the screen slammed shut behind me. I stormed out of our front yard, almost running to separate myself in some way from the tension dwelling in my home.

I just had to get out and walk! Walking helped me to clear my head. Walking settled my mind and gave me space to breathe and pray. And pray I did! It seemed like I did so unceasingly, but also my prayers seemed to never go any further than my own mind. But praying still made me feel better.

"Do you not hear me, God? I know you do but I am just so weary of it all."

Turning the corner, I settled in a rhythm with my walking. My gait was calmer now. My heart wasn't racing anymore. I blinked and tried to keep the tears back, but they began to fall like rain down my flushed cheeks. Brushing them off my face, I tasted their saltiness and thanked God. Yes, He has heard my many prayers. He had begun softening my hard heart. Those salty tears were proof of His love and mercy, but I was still weary of trying to hold it all together while I watched everything falling apart.

Walking down the familiar path to the waters of the bayou where I lived, I gathered up speed. I knew I would begin to feel much better when I finally got there.

There was an old oak tree growing near the shore of the bayou, and over the years its roots grew long and strong as they anchored themselves to the sandy beach soil. They became like strong arms for me to sit on while I cried and poured out my heart to God. It was quiet there. It was beautiful there, and I felt better by just sitting there on the strong arms of the oak tree near the water's edge of my beautiful Beach Haven bayou.

It's funny that I have lived near this spot for as long as I can remember. As a child, I grew up only five minutes from there. Then when we moved back to Pensacola from Denver, we rented a house also five minutes from there, and now that I was in my early 30s, here we were again, living in a rented house five minutes from the same spot!

I cried a barrel of tears sitting on these strong oak tree arms. I was weary, though, of waiting for His answers. Even with all my praying, things seemed to get worse rather than better.

"Help me to understand, Lord. Perhaps I'm not praying correctly. Is that it, Lord? Teach me how to pray."

Sitting there alone in the arms of my praying tree, a slight burst of light entered my soul. Awareness took hold of my thoughts. Maybe my prayers have been wrong somehow: "Show me, Father. Teach me, Lord."

Sitting there watching the beautiful glow of the sunset over the waters of the still bayou, I could sense the peace of God settling my heart.

"Get up, Thea, go home and pray ... not by asking but by giving. It is in giving that you receive.

"Come to me with open hands. Pry your needy fingers off what you want 'too much' and just trust that I know what is best. Pray only for My will to be done. Pray forgiving others and walk in humility accepting everything from My hand. Trust in My promise that I am always with you and will work all this out for My glory and your good.

"You have 'disordered loves.' My gifts of home and family have been your greatest desire. You have wanted My gifts more than Me. It is your heart I've been after because in loving Me above all else, you will then be happy and no one can ever take that from you. I AM always to be your greatest delight."

Slowly I got up from the water's edge and began my walk home carrying with me a mustard seed of faith within my wounded but healing heart.

Let it go, Thea.

God knows it all.

God cares and understands.

He will always do what is best for His children.

Do not fret or be anxious for anything. Fear not.

Thank Him for everything, even with salty tears running down your face: "I see it now, Lord; with empty hands I surrender, now ready for whatever You place there. Thy will be done!"

"Whenever I am afraid, I will trust in You. In God I will praise His Word. In God have I put my trust, I will not fear, what can flesh do to me? You number my wanderings; Put my tears in Your bottle; Are they not in Your book when I cry out to You? Be merciful to me O God,

be merciful to me! For my soul trusts in You. And in the shadow of Your wings I will make my refuge until these calamities have passed by" (Psalm 56:3-4, 8; 57:1).

30
Living in the Wake

SOBBING UNCONTROLLABLY, I hardly noticed my front door open. Hearing footsteps, I looked up and saw her small frame standing in my living room.

Sitting down next to me on the couch, she softly patted my knee and whispered, "Thea, calm down … calm down … it's going to be alright." I laid my head on her lap and continued to cry, a little less terrified now that she was with me.

I was caught in the wake of alcoholism, and I was drowning. Emotionally bruised and battered, hanging on by a thread, she walked into my dark maze of a life and offered me hope.

She had heard it all before, many times, and offered help, but as crazy as it sounds, I refused to take her advice. The medicine she offered my sick soul did not taste good.

I often thought that addictions were like big beautiful shiny cigarette boats! They are so alluring and exciting when you first get in, cruising out on the water, speeding your way through the sun and the surf, the wind blowing through your hair, everything flying by in a blur. Life is exciting, but somehow, over time, you lose control and now you are stuck behind a steering wheel that you can't control. The cigarette boat is going crazy, doing its own thing at wildly excessive speeds. You are trapped ... a cigarette boat prisoner! You are shackled by a rope ... one end holding you captive in the boat, the other end hanging over the back of the boat, being tossed about in the angry foam of the wake.

And attached to the end of that rope are all the people who love the prisoner of the out-of-control cigarette boat.

They are trapped too ... in your wake.

I had been wakeboarding for years, and that day, I was ready to let go of the rope.

My mother sat there patting my back until I calmed down and stopped crying.

I really just wanted to be her little girl again. I wanted to crawl up into her soft lap and let her sing to me while she rocked me in my grandmother's old maple rocking chair. I wanted my mother to make the pain go away like she used to when I fell down and skinned my knee.

But I was a grown woman in my 30s with three children so that wasn't going to happen!

You see, my mother knew the answer to my problem. She had offered it to me before, but it wasn't what I wanted so I dismissed it and continued my wakeboarding life.

But that day, after a culmination of problems, I broke. I could feel my grip on the wakeboarding rope begin to loosen and finally, I let it go.

You may think my mother took my side, listened to my woes and told me that I deserved better, but that is NOT what she said. She was much too wise for that. She was not into the quick-fix, poor-me, philosophy of life. She knew that the medicine I needed for my sick soul was so much greater than that!

Did I want more peace in my life? My answer: "Yes, yes I do."

I had been a Christian for over 10 years, but peace is not what you feel when you live life as a wakeboarder.

But that day, that's what I wanted. That's what I desperately needed ... peace ... God's peace.

I knew my mother loved me and had spent years grieving over my painful life. I knew she had cried a bucket of tears as she carried me to the Lord in prayer, but she could not do for me what I needed to do for myself. So once again, she offered me the medicine I so desperately needed.

"Thea, your life is never going to improve until you start your day on your knees, surrendering all to God, and get into His Holy Word. Only He can give you what you need. He is the answer to your life."

And so I did. I let go of one rope, trying to control what I had no control over, and received another invisible rope, tied to the sure and certain Word of God.

Oh, I was still connected to the out-of-control cigarette boat named alcoholism, but I was not caught in its wake anymore. I was tethered to the captain of my soul. I heard His voice— "Peace, be still"—and the raging wind in my own soul began to quiet down.

It's been more than 30 years since that day in my living room with my mother. I took the medicine she offered and began right away, doing exactly what she told me to do. And, oh, the healing that began in my own tortured soul.

In 2 Peter 1:1-15 (Life Application Bible), we read, "From Simon Peter, a servant and missionary of Jesus Christ. To all of you who have our kind of faith. The faith I speak of is the kind that Jesus Christ our God and Savior gives to us. How precious it is, and how just and good He is to give this same kind of faith to each of us. Do you want more and more of God's kindness and peace? Then learn to know Him better and better. For as you know Him better, He will give you, through his great power, everything you need for living a truly good life; He even shares His own glory and His own goodness with us. And by that same mighty power He has given us all the other rich and wonderful blessings He promised; for instance, the promise to save us from the lust and rottenness all around us and to give us His own character.

But to obtain these gifts, you need more than faith; you must also work hard to be good and even that is not enough. For then you must learn to know God better and discover what He wants you to do. Next, learn to put aside your own desires so that you will become patient and godly, gladly letting God have His way with you. This will make possible the next step; which is for you to enjoy other people and to like them and finally you will grow to love them deeply. The more you go in this way, the more you will grow strong spiritually and become fruitful and useful to the Lord Jesus Christ. But anyone who fails to go after these additions to faith is blind indeed, or at least very short-sighted, and has forgotten that God delivered him from the old life of sin so that now he can live a strong, good life for the Lord. So, dear brothers, work hard to prove that you really are counted among those God has called and chosen and then you will never stumble or fall away. And God will open wide the gates of heaven for you to enter into the eternal kingdom of our

Lord and Savior Jesus Christ. I plan to keep on reminding you of these things though you already know them and are really getting along quite well! But the Lord Jesus Christ has showed me that my days here on earth are numbered and I am soon to die. As long as I am still here I intend to keep sending these reminders to you hoping to impress them so clearly upon you that you will remember them long after I am gone."

My little mother, kept reminding me of the TRUTH of where real peace and joy come from ... NOT from the absence of problems but from knowing the Lord through His Word.

I did not realize that day in my living room that she was in the beginning stages of Alzheimer's. Time was short, and very soon I would no longer enjoy her loving touches of comfort and wisdom. She would begin to fade as the disease took hold of her mind.

Just like the apostle Peter kept reminding those he loved how to follow in faith, my mother kept reminding me until she faded away into the arms of TRUTH Himself!

Thank you, mother; I remember. I am still anchored to the rope, I am still getting to know Him better and better through His Word.

"I am continually with you; You hold my right hand. You guide me with Your counsel and afterward You will receive me to glory. Whom have I in heaven but You? And there is nothing on earth that I desire besides You. My flesh and my heart may fail, but God is the strength of my heart and my portion forever" (Psalm 73:23-26).

"Jesus answered, 'I am the WAY and the TRUTH and the LIFE. No one comes to the Father except through Me'" (John 14:6).

"*My soul continually remembers it and is bowed down within me. But this I call to mind, and therefore I have hope. The steadfast love of the Lord never ceases; His mercies never come to an end; they are new every morning; great is Your faithfulness. The Lord is my portion, says my soul, therefore I will hope in Him. The Lord is good to those who wait for him, to the soul who seeks Him. It is good that one should wait quietly for the salvation of the Lord*" (Lamentations 3:20-25).

31
A Tangled Mess

IT WAS A chilly Saturday morning in mid-December. Throwing a sweatshirt over my pajamas I slowly walked out to the garage, sipping my mug of hot coffee.

I felt hollow that morning, like an empty shell … numb, drained. I mustered all my strength even to walk to the garage as wet tears welled up in my eyes … again.

My house was empty. All three of my children were gone for the weekend. The emptiness of the house haunted me. The silent walls screamed with a voice I heard too often in my head: "Thea, you have failed again."

Trying to ignore the voice in my mind, I walked over to the large cupboard in the garage where I kept all my Christmas decorations.

My plan for that weekend was to get my house decorated for Christmas before my kids came home.

Trying desperately to get into the holiday spirit, I opened the large cupboard door and just stared at all the boxes labeled "CHRISTMAS." It was really such a farce! My heart was void of all Christmas cheer —all my heart felt was the empty wasteland of … "Why, God? Why here at Christmastime?"

I began pulling down the cardboard boxes and hauling them into the family room. One after another I lugged the big boxes inside and set them in the corner of the room. Feeling extremely exhausted, I sat down in my mother's old rocking chair that's now mine and stared at the fire I built earlier in the fireplace. I can still smell the pine from the lighter wood I used to start the fire. Burning pine always reminds me of my daddy. Tears fell again as I thought about him. I wished my daddy were still alive; he would have known what to do.

Watching the flames consume the remaining firewood, I felt like one of the logs, unable to remove myself from the fire, all the while the fire consuming the wood and turning everything to dust.

Rocking back and forth in the arms of mother's rocker, I cried out to God, "Help me; I can't take this pain anymore. Please God, my heart is broken beyond repair, and I feel like my whole life is turning into dust and nothing makes sense to me. Nothing … nothing but You."

Walking back to into the garage, I stooped down and opened the last cabinet drawer … the drawer I had avoided ever since I made the decision to put up the Christmas decorations.

Slowly, I opened the deep drawer and stared at the tangled mess. I don't know why I do this to myself every year. I guess I'm just impatient. My mother always told me I needed to practice patience, but I didn't want to! I didn't like to wait. I had things to do! She used to say, "Thea, the hurrier you go, the behinder you get." I usually just laughed at her.

Staring again at the tangled mess, I remembered when I threw all these Christmas lights in a big box without separating them. Thinking back to last Christmas, it was nice. My son was a senior in high school. Little did I realize it was to be the last Christmas our family of five would ever celebrate together.

Now, a year later, I sat alone in the garage of our rented house and stared at the cobweb of green plastic wires and tiny plastic bulbs. If I had the money, I'd just throw them all away and go buy new ones, but I didn't, so I started pulling out the big wad of twisted lights.

My patience was gone before I even got started, but slowly I began pulling apart each string of lights. After about 10 minutes of frustrated fighting, salty tears once again fell down into my lap full of plastic light bulbs.

In an instant, I felt a nudge from the Holy Spirit ... I remembered a scripture verse: "I will bless the Lord at all times, His praise will be forever on my lips" (Psalm 34:1). Slowly, I started singing to myself songs of praise I learned at my mother's knees. Often, all I could sing was "Jesus loves me, this I know, for the Bible tells me so." Singing of Jesus moved my thoughts to the real meaning of Christmas. It's NOT all about family! "Jesus came to save His people from their sin" (Matthew 1:21). I'm one of His people—save me Jesus from my sin of self-pity and resentment.

As I continued to untangle the Christmas lights, I realized they were a picture of my life. Every year, in my impatience, I just threw the lights back in a box without taking the time to sort through and re-organize them for the next year. "I'll do it later," I would say, but later never came, so each year I dealt with the same frustrating problems. I do that with so many of my problems, just stuff them away in a secret place in my heart and hope they go away. They don't.

I was realizing in all my pain and prayer and solitude that God was unraveling ME and it hurt. I had to learn to sit still and surrender as the potter remade his little lump of clay named Thea.

I prayed, "Yes, Lord, I do what You want, even if I complain and cry. You know that in the deepest place of my heart You have placed a settled willingness to surrender to Your will, whatever that is. Hesitantly, I welcome Your hand of grace into all the deep and secret places of my heart that I've tried so hard to keep hidden."

Finally getting the strings of lights separated and all the bulbs working, I dragged them into the family room in preparation to place them on our artificial Christmas tree that I had set up in the far corner of the room. Those colorful bright lights would make our old tree look beautiful!

Yes, Christmas would definitely be different from the Christmases of the past 20 years. Sadder, yes, but in a strange way, more peaceful. Did I know what my future would hold? NO! Did I have money saved up to help me as a new single mom? NO! Did I know what I was going to do? Absolutely NOT!

But God in his refining mercy stripped away my mask of self-will and let me feel the freedom of weakness and helplessness. I was learning HOW to depend on God alone—day by day, moment by moment. He was really all I needed.

I thought, "The Lord is my Shepherd and He is leading me to green pastures and still waters. He will restore my soul. I'm confident that He will straighten ME out and then maybe one day, my life can be like one of these tiny bright bulbs on my

Christmas tree, letting my light shine for the glory of the re-storing God!" But for that moment, I figured I would just lie in my dark family room and look up at all the beautiful sparkling lights on my old artificial tree! And rest … singing softly to my-self … "This little light of mine, I'm going to let it shine, let it shine, let it shine, let it shine!"

"When my spirit was overwhelmed within me, then You knew my path, in the way in which I walked. For there is no one who acknowl-edges me. Refuge has failed me. No one cares for my soul. I cried out to You Lord; I said, You are my refuge, my portion in the land of the liv-ing, attend to my cry. For I am brought very low; deliver me from my persecutors for they are stronger than I. Bring my soul out of prison, that I may praise Your name. Cause me to hear Your lovingkindness in the morning, for in You do I trust. Cause me to know the way in which I should walk, for I lift up my soul to You. Teach me to do Your will, for You are my God. Your Spirit is good; lead me in the land of uprightness. Revive me, O Lord for Your Name's sake! For Your righteousness's sake bring my soul out of trouble! I will extol You, my God, my King; and I will bless Your name forever" (Sections from Psalm 142, 143 and 145).

Reliving this memory and putting those thoughts into words on a page forced me to look at myself with eyes of grace that only come through my Lord and Savior; without this grace, this story would have become very depressing! I'd been a Chris-tian for many years at that time, but I was just on the edge of learning what it meant to live by faith and not by sight. I had a degree in denial and a master's degree in self-will and determination! Pain shattered that delusion and grace led me into seeking the face of God in His Word for healing that only He could give me. I knew my heart was broken beyond repair and my inner soul (my mind, emotions and will) were also sick and getting sicker by the year. Only God could heal me, and He did.

He took my feeble hand and led me down a path of wisdom so I could understand Him more and face myself, then walked with me upward into the path of joy in His presence. It was right after this experience with the Christmas lights that I was introduced to the wisdom of the serenity prayer:

"God, grant me the grace and serenity, to accept what I cannot change, courage to change what I can and the wisdom to know the difference. Living one day at a time, enjoying one moment at a time, accepting hardship as the pathway to peace, taking as Jesus did, this sinful world as it is, not as I would have it. Trusting that You will make all things right, if I surrender to Your will, so that I may be reasonably happy in this life and supremely happy with YOU forever in the next."

Yes, it was a long walk and many times very painful, but He held my hand as He shined His light into the secret places of myself I'd never ventured to examine. And He changed me. He freed me from my chains of denial, fear, and pride in my own self-will that I could change anything! Over time, I learned to be content and walk in peace and joy … Christ IN me, my only hope of glory! In writing these stories over this last year, I placed myself in my head and relived many, many memories. Some good, some bad, as life is!

All I can do is praise Him: "Thank you Lord, for Your hand

of grace on me, before I was born, while I was growing up, while I was self-willed and rebellious running from You, while I was lonely and hurting, sick and deceived. You saw me, You came and You did just what You said you would do. Jesus came to save His people from their sin! Once on the cross of Calvary, and then every day a fresh cleansing as You continually sanctify me until the day I leave this earth and wake up in heaven, no longer walking by faith, but by sight." I will see HIM face to face.

Until then, I am still looking to Jesus, the author and finisher of my faith! For He has made me GLAD!

32
From Garbage to Glory
(Hint, Hint: This Is the Story of My Life)

SQUATTING DOWN ON the long dusty trail next to my wheelbarrow, I slowly started picking up garbage.

Broken eggshells, coffee filters filled with wet coffee grinds, smelly scraps from the frozen fish sticks my kids didn't eat several nights ago … it all disgusted me! I grabbed the garbage and threw it back into my wheelbarrow and began my journey again to the end of the empty field where my landlord had his burn pile.

I tripped when my foot was caught in a large hole hidden by the tall weeds in the field, spilling everything in the wheelbarrow as I fell to the ground.

Hot tears rolling down my face, inhaling the putrid smell of my own garbage, I cried with each step along the long trail.

It was a very cold and dismal day in December. I used to love the month of Christmas, but that year I hated it. My cold fingers were burning now from picking up all the wet garbage.

All I really wanted to do was throw down all the garbage and run away! Run away from everything! Run away from my life and run back home to my mama. Run back to the home I grew up in, where I felt loved, safe and secure.

I just wanted to be my mama's little girl again and sit in her lap and hear her tell me, "It's going to be alright, Thea." I wanted to hear her sing "God will take care of you!"

At the same time, as I was thinking about my mother's voice singing to me, another truth jumped into the forefront of my mind.

"Thea, are you thanking Me for this garbage?"

"Really, God? You want me to thank You for THIS? Thank you for this horrible mess I'm in and now, literally, thank You for the mess of all this spilled garbage? Really?"

I was a single mom, struggling to survive another day, going through a divorce after 23 years of marriage.

I felt like my life was one big pile of garbage spilled everywhere, and I was secretly mad at God for not answering my prayers to save my marriage.

The thought jumped back into my mind again, "Are you thanking ME for all things like I taught you to do? Do you remember what I said in 1 Thessalonians 5:15-18, 'See to it that no one repays evil for evil but do good to one another and to everyone. Rejoice always, pray without ceasing, give thanks in ALL circumstances; for this is the will of God in Christ Jesus for you'?"

Dropping my head and drying off my tears with my coat sleeve, I quietly spoke these words into the air: "Thank you, Lord, for all things, even this messy garbage I find myself in; I know You are the Sovereign God. You never change and You are in control, even though NOTHING makes sense to me. Thy will be done."

Immediately, after the last hushed word left my mouth, like a bolt of lightning barging into my brain, six beautiful words overpowered my whining mind: "You forgot to wash your hands!"

Stopping dead in my tracks, alone in the big empty field, hauling my garbage to be burned, I just stood there FROZEN!

It was bitter cold, but I could feel myself becoming flushed as if heat was surging through my inner self.

With enthusiasm I yelled, "Yes, I forgot to wash my hands!"

Tears began to flow again but this time, they were tears of joy!

Laughing and crying at the same time, I left the wheelbarrow and started running back up the trail, back to my rented house, singing those words to myself!

"Thank You, Lord; I forgot to wash my hands! Thank You, Lord; I forgot to wash my hands!"

Finally, arriving at the beginning of the trail at the back door of my landlord's garage, I threw open the door and ran over to the large, deep stainless steel sink and began washing my hands.

I tasted my salty tears as I sang my new little song of praise and felt the warm water running over my cold and burning fingers.

Drying my hands off with a paper towel, I sat down on a stool in the garage and stared at the piece of furniture I had been refinishing.

Trying to remain positive through all the messiness I had gone through, I busied myself refinishing furniture, which had become one of my pastimes.

That morning after my kids left for school, I worked on a piece of furniture, stripping all the gunk off to expose the beautiful oak wood underneath. Dirty from all the gunk, I used gasoline to clean off all the sticky black stuff from my hands!

Energized in my own "gunk" of self-pity, I had thoughtlessly grabbed the big box of wooden matches and headed out to the burn pile without washing my hands.

One strike of that wooden kitchen match and my hands would have gone up in flames!

I forgot to wash my hands!

Sitting there on that stool alone in my landlord's garage, all I could do was cry and praise Him from whom all blessings flow.

That day was a turning point in my life!

I realized that day that when I looked at life through my own set of glasses that, oftentimes, life just "sucked"!

Shattered dreams, unanswered prayers, enormous lacks, unending fears—all wanted to consume my head and drown me in self-pity!

My own negative thoughts lied to me over and over again; like the skipping beat of an old, scratched vinyl record, they played the same message over and over again: "You are alone. God doesn't care. You'll never make it so you might as well give up!"

Lies, all lies!

Until He helped me remember His words …

I could not hear the sweet and gentle prompting of the Holy Spirit until His words smashed the lies I wallowed around in and then obeyed what His Word told me to do! Feelings had nothing to do with it!

"Rejoice in the Lord, pray without ceasing and in ALL things give thanks, for this IS the will of God IN Christ Jesus for you" (1 Thessalonians 5:16-18).

As I think of myself as the chubby little tan girl who loved to sit in my mother's lap and have her rock me and sing to me, I also remember her as the little girl who lived in her "pretend world" where she thought she was the BOSS of her life.

I'm NOT the boss of my life, or anyone else's life, or my thoughts … or anything else!

I'm not God! I need a continual reminder of that, and the best way is to just keep remembering what His Word tells me to do: keep on praying, praising, rejoicing and thanking Him!

When I'm doing that I am quiet inside, and I have ears to hear the voice of the Good Shepherd leading His mixed-up but loved little sheep named Thea, who really doesn't understand anything!

And I don't need to understand anything right now because God does and that's enough!

Broken, I cried out to Him in praise and thanksgiving, "Thank You, thank You, Lord! Let those words be the cry of my heart until I see You one day … face to face! I do believe; help my unbelief!"

"See that no one repays anyone evil for evil, but always seek to do good to one another and to everyone. Rejoice always, pray without ceasing, give thanks in ALL circumstances; for this IS the will of God in Christ Jesus for you. Do not quench the Spirit" (1 Thessalonians 5:15-19).

"With tears flowing, the child's father at once cried out, I do believe; help my unbelief" (Mark 9:24).

"From the rising of the sun unto the setting of the same, the Lord's name is to be praised" (Psalm 113:3).

.

33
The Blessing of Possessing Nothing

STANDING AT THE kitchen sink washing the breakfast dishes, I heard the voice of my son who was home from college: "Mom, what happened? The water just stopped!" He was in the shower.

Frantic, I didn't know. I didn't know much of anything. I was new to this life as a single mom and found myself jumping into panic mode at each new turn of events.

I always paid my bills. My income was very small so I carefully watched every penny I spent, so I thought I had paid my water bill.

Grabbing the phone, I called the water company, hoping the trouble was with them. The curt woman on the phone said, "No, your bill is delinquent, and you will need to come down here today and pay the balance and also a hook-up fee."

Hurriedly getting dressed, I grabbed my checkbook and jumped into the car, asking my son to keep an eye on his two little sisters while I was gone. I enjoyed seeing his smiling face standing in the doorway. I missed him terribly while he was away at Florida State.

Taking a quick look at my checkbook, I realized how little money there was. I had purposely kept that money aside
for groceries that next week. Backing my car into the highway
traffic, my panic blossomed into crying. It seemed I cried all
the time, but I was glad, because for years I never cried; I only
shoved things down and my heart grew hard. Those tears had
definitely been a source of release with all the stress of my life.

I started singing and thanking God. This was the only way
I could cope with anything. I started thanking God, reminding
myself that He was in control and not me. I sang to myself as
I usually did, with tears and a red face. Sitting at a red light, I
was afraid to look at the person in the car next to me ... does
he notice the crazy woman who is crying and singing? It didn't
matter; I wasn't talking to him anyway.

Parking my car at the water company, I dried my face, reapplied my lipstick, went inside, took a seat and waited my turn.
Within a few minutes, I heard my name and slowly walked over
and sat in front of an attractive 30-something black woman.
She smiled kindly and asked me what happened. I explained
it all. She checked my records and yes, I must have missed that
month's payment somehow, but if I could take care of it that
day, she would have it turned back on right away.

Managing a small smile, I thanked her and thanked the Lord
and began rehearsing to her how hard this new life as a single
mom had been and how praising God for all things helped me
remain calm and keep trusting the Lord. Immediately, her eyes
welled up in tears and she quickly reached across her desk and
grabbed my arm. Trying to keep her tears back, her lip quivering, she said, "I know the real reason your water was turned

off—it was God! God sent you to me today!"

She began rehearsing her story: she was also a single mom with three kids and life was very, very difficult. She had no one to turn to. She had prayed and worried all night long. Very early that morning she had gotten on her knees and prayed, "God, if You are there, if You can hear me, please send me a sign today. I need something." By this time, we were both crying! I reassured her that He does know and He cares and He is all she needs. I encouraged her to read her Bible and plug into a good church and just keep praising God. She smiled and thanked me profusely and we hugged ... newfound sisters in Christ.

I sang all the way home—not through frantic tears but with my outside loud and happy voice! I still didn't know how I would make it that next week with an empty checking account, but I knew somehow God would take care of me as He always did!

The weekend came and went, and we waved as the number 1 son and best big brother in the world returned to FSU. My little girls went to school and I went to work, still lingering in the joy of being used by God in such a glorious way to help another struggling young woman.

Finally, at the end of the day, pulling into our driveway with little girls in tow, I noticed a big sign taped to the garage door. Rushing to the sign, I read it with a little apprehension. It was from a good friend. His older sister ran an elderly care facility in town. The company she buys food from had made a mistake and sent way more than they could store in their freezer, so this woman called our friend to ask if he knew anyone who could use some frozen food. Pulling the garage door open and rushing to the big freezer my landlord said I could use, I opened the door and just started crying again! From top to bottom it was filled with assorted frozen foods! I was overwhelmed and walked into the house, praising the Lord, from whom all blessings flow!

Later that night after my girls had gone to bed, I sat down and looked at the mail. There was a beautiful pink card addressed to me. I had many friends, and it helped so much to get cards of encouragement while I was getting adjusted to being a single mom. Opening the card, I could hardly believe what I saw. A sweet note that said, "The Lord impressed upon me that you could use a little help this month, with much love!" I was holding a check for $1,500 with my name on it. All I could do was sit and cry again, tears of grateful joy!

That night, snuggled up in my warm bed, I was crying again and feeling like Mary, the woman who sat at the feet of Jesus and drank in His words: "This is my comfort in my affliction, Your Word gives me life." *Oh, how I love You, Lord.* Softly I sang to myself, "God will take care of you, through every day, through every way, He will take care of you … God will take care of you!"

"The Lord will continually lead you; He will feed you even in parched regions. He will give you renewed strength and you will be like a well-watered garden, like a spring that continually produces water" (Isaiah 58:11).

34
Laundry Baskets and Lightning Bugs

OVERWHELMED WITH LAUNDRY, I sat and perused the unending mountain of clothes.

It seemed that no matter how hard I tried to stay up with the mound, it rose like lava from a volcano! It drained me!

I had been a single mom for several years, with two cute little girls at home. My son was a student at Florida State University and was home only on holidays.

My house was cute and almost storybook-like. Everything was dainty for the three little girls who lived in the house. There were teddy bears and frilly pillows everywhere. My couch was just a very small loveseat that I found at a thrift store … what do three little girls need with a big couch anyway?

I had recently remarried to a minister with two boys of his own.

It was love at first sight for both of us, and we were married in just over 50 days from the first time we laid eyes on each other.

I was not prepared for it! Definitely NOT prepared!

I worked full time in a dental office and had taken on another full-time job: pastor's wife and stepmom.

How does one prepare to be a pastor's wife? How do you prepare yourself to go from washing little girls' delicate clothes to big boy clothes that fill up your washing machine with just their jeans?

It seemed like the mountain of laundry I faced every few days reminded me of my inadequacy. No matter how hard I tried, I just couldn't get it under control. I hated it. I dreaded it. Inwardly, I complained to God about all the extra work I had to do. I dared not tell anyone else because I loved my new family and I wanted to take care of all their needs and be really good at both: pastor's wife and stepmom! But it was hard … really hard. And I was getting tired … really tired.

My new pastor husband seemed to read me pretty well; although perhaps it was wisdom from above that convinced him to suggest we take a vacation!

A vacation? We didn't have the money to take a vacation! I could only get off from work for a week, and vacations took planning and money, of which we had neither!

He planned anyway, and somehow a little extra money appeared.

We were going camping in the mountains! A completely new adventure for my little girls.

We discussed our family vacation at dinnertime around the table. His boys had been camping before, and they began painting the picture of an adventure of a lifetime for their two new little stepsisters! They were eager and quite gullible. We borrowed a large tent, found sleeping bags for everyone, discussed what we would cook over the open flame—could we roast wieners on sticks and make s'mores?

The day finally arrived, and we all squeezed into our van, which was loaded down with camping gear!

After a long trip hearing "Are we there yet?" a million times, we finally arrived at Roane Mountain Campground, a short drive from Gatlinburg, Tennessee.

It was absolutely beautiful! My husband's planning had paid off, and our campsite was breathtaking. We were nestled between low-hanging evergreens and a stream that ran through the campground. Trying to get our kids to help us unpack was almost impossible. Having been cooped up in the van for so long, the call of the wild was almost more than they could bear!

Finally, after emptying the van, we released them to go exploring! The big brothers led the way, and their new little sisters eagerly followed down to the creek!

Out of the corner of my eye, I saw my little girls following their new big brothers over large boulders and rapid running waters! "Be careful," I yelled! They were in heaven!

My husband, with some previous experience in camping, knew just how to set things up. Following his lead, in only a few hours we had our new home away from home organized. It was wonderful.

It took me awhile to begin to feel it. Camping was new to me, and it had been a lot of work so far, but I sensed something happening: an awareness of peace seemed to fill the air, like the fresh scent of the evergreens above us, a stillness that was only broken by the sound of the rushing water and the laughter of our children below.

It started slowly, very slowly, but it was real. God's presence was there … in the woods.

Our first night was amazing: cooking hamburgers and hot dogs on an open-fire pit; kids laughing at each other; big brothers teasing little sisters with each strange sound that pierced the darkness; little sisters coaxing big brothers to let them braid their hair, tying it off with colorful little barrettes; big brothers swearing little sisters to secrecy!

The days were filled with kids riding their bicycles round and round the campgrounds to see if they could find some new friends, and teenage boys finally finding really cute girls to flirt with at the ping-pong table in the rec room. (We were forever wondering where those boys were!)

My husband, loving to live on the edge, decided he wanted to take his bike up to the top of the mountain and then coast down. What a rush! But not for this girl! Slowly riding through the bike trail of the campground was enough for me. The scents, the rhododendron, the sound of the rapids from the creek below were thrill enough for me.

After an overload of sugar from our s'mores, the kids winding down, staring at the bonfire, it was finally quiet. The day had ended. Mesmerized by the crackling fire and lightning bugs darting above us, the stillness continued to roll in like the mist of the night.

On our last night at the campground, the end of our vacation, zipping up our big tent with all six of us packed in like sardines, I snuggled up to my husband and said, "Thank you."

It was a great vacation, and I think our kids will forever remember the fun we had!

I had been drowning in my laundry and in my imagination that I couldn't do everything.

I couldn't … and still can't. He knew that.

Yes, times have changed. There is no longer a little story-book house with delicate girly clothes and only doing laundry on Saturdays. There are men around with big appetites and big clothes and laundry every day! There is church work, church work, and more church work. There is way too much to do in the 24 hours of the day.

Aha moment: I don't have to do it all!

I just need to stay in the Presence of the Lord so I can listen to His instructions for the day. He is much kinder to me … than me.

When Jesus lived on this earth, He did not solve everyone's problems. The government was still corrupt; there was still leprosy and poor people everywhere. He healed many, helped many but at night He knew He had done what His Father wanted Him to do for that day. He could rest.

The rest doesn't come because all the bills are paid or because the kids got all A's on their report cards or because the laundry is all finished. Peace is a person and He is realized as you spend time in His presence. Peace is hearing His voice in His Word. It's living in the NOW with Him, knowing He is enough. He is always enough.

That's how you learn to be a pastor's wife or a mom or a stepmom or anything else you are called to do. You can't really prepare for it, you just have to spend time at His feet, daily drinking in His Word. He will give what you need, when you need it. Peace is there, He is there, even as you are counting the blessings of another five baskets of clothes to fold!

I started folding again and hummed:

"Count Your Blessings"

Count your blessings, name them one by one;
Count your blessings, see what God has done.
Count your blessings, name them one by one;
Count your many blessings, see what God has done.
And it will surprise you what the Lord has done.

"Not that I am speaking of being in need, for I have learned in whatever situation I am to be content. I know how to be brought low and I know how to abound. In any and every circumstance, I have learned the secret of facing plenty and hunger, abundance and need. I can do all things through Him who strengthens me" (Philippians 4:11-13).

35

Living in Plan B Grace

SLIPPING MY FEET out from under my warm comforter, I slid into my furry slippers next to the bed and headed to the kitchen. It was still dark outside, and the house had a chill to it. I stopped in the hallway and turned up the thermostat.

I'm an early riser, but that morning I woke before my alarm went off. I think I was just excited about the day and eager to get started!

Flipping on the light switch in the kitchen, I went to the sink to fill up the coffeepot and wait.

Grabbing my Bible, my many prayer books and my journal, I balanced my hot cup of coffee and dragged myself into the dark living room, sitting carefully on one end of the couch. Turning on a small lamp, I silently enjoyed the circle of light I found myself in on that cold morning in late November.

Slowly I sipped my hot coffee and looked down the dark hallway where all the people I love so much were snuggled up and sleeping in their respective bedrooms. Their doors were closed, and the house was silent.

It was Thanksgiving Day. This is the first Thanksgiving for our new blended family.

Those last five months had been some of the happiest times in my life and for this I was overwhelmingly grateful! My life had entered into a new journey that I would never, ever in a million years thought I would travel! Divorced after 23 years of marriage, I had gotten married to a minister with kids of his own! That day our little 900-square-foot home was housing five children behind three closed bedroom doors!

The "D" word (divorce) was something I never thought would happen to me, but it did, and I often thought, "Where did things go wrong?"

After your world has been shattered, hopefully you gain some wisdom and become better from it and not bitter. I opted for the better part and put all my hopes and dreams in the Lord, the only perfect One!

I was my parents' only divorced child.

My parents enjoyed a long and happy marriage, and I was blessed to have that as my family heritage. As they graduated into their senior-citizen love, they were so cute with each other. I would catch them dancing in the kitchen when an old waltz would play on the radio. I remember watching my father sitting on the couch, holding my mother's hand. They loved each other, and they knew "how" to love each other. They learned to connect the dots with love in action. I never, ever heard them fight or even raise their voice at one another. I could see the way my daddy looked at my mother when she was all dressed up for church. My daddy stuttered slightly so he didn't talk much, but he would smile his little squinty-eyed smile and say, "You look nice." She had that little sparkle in her eye when she smiled back at him with a look that said, "I know you're a man of few words, but I know you love me." It was adorable. They were high school sweethearts and remained that way until they died!

I don't know when I grasped the fact that I had never loved like that or that I probably never would. I accepted that a love like theirs was not my lot in life, and that was OK. I kept seeking after God, the only real perfect Love.

And His love found me. Later, I realized the only reason I was seeking Him was because He was seeking me first. The early morning seeking became for me an ushering into a secret place of love and prayer beyond my previous comprehension! I tasted the sweetness of the Word of God: "The ordinances of the Lord are sweeter than honey and drippings of honeycomb" (Psalm 19:8).

I finally realized that God had touched my heart so radically and filled my heart with so much of His love that I wondered why I'd searched for it in mere humans. There is no other source except Him—not a spouse or a child or success or possessions or good health. God's love is so much greater than anything this world has to offer, and His love never ends!

I was satisfied with knowing God. I was at peace because He knew me. I was not helpless or alone because his Word spoke to me when I read it with a seeking heart. He is enough! His love is the only love that can truly satisfy the human heart. I was content.

And then, out of the blue, an unexpected miracle happened!

One sunny day in the springtime, my girls and I were invited to the baptism of a friend. Making our way to the front of the church, we sat down and waited for the pastor to proceed with the service. Baptisms are always thrilling when you see a person demonstrate, in the water, what has actually taken place in their heart. We were happy for our friend! The young pastor's preaching was powerful. He spoke as one who had also been broken. We rose from our seats for the final prayer of blessing and dismissal. Closing my eyes and looking toward heaven, as was my habit, I prayed, and the young single pastor heard in his heart the voice of God: "Don, there she is!"

He said he took one look at my face while I was praying and said, "Yes, Lord, I want her!"

The rest is history. We were married in just over 50 days from that moment!

Two broken people shattered by divorce, two broken families now bound together tenderly by the sweet and humble hands of the Healer and our Savior, Christ Jesus, the Redeemer and the Restorer of the broken-hearted.

I'd never experienced such love as I did from this preacher man, Don Coker.

The only thing I can attribute it to is that we both loved God more than any other. Our hearts had once been shattered, our worlds had turned upside down, but our relationship with the Lord deepened. The trials brought us both a new appreciation for the love of God IN Christ Jesus our Lord.

God gave us a gift of grace—each other to each other. We knew by theology and by experience that a mere human can never be our greatest love but only a gift on loan from the source of love, God Himself.

And with this gift of grace came other gifts, children: my three, Phil, Heidi and Gretchen, and his two, Jason and Jeff. The dark hallway ahead, with its closed bedroom doors, housed these precious souls … our newly blended children.

I realized very quickly that these children did not fall in love; they just had to come along with their parents. Now they were living in a strange home, not theirs, with a strange parent, also not theirs. All alone, wondering in their silent thoughts behind these closed doors, "What happened to MY family?"

And I also wondered, "What will become of these precious ones we love so much?"

Behind these doors, in my dark hallway, lay children who had been hurt. Hurt by the ones who should never hurt them … but did. Their little hearts were broken and I could already see the walls of protective barriers they were building to guard themselves from more inward pain.

No one can go through a divorce and come away unscathed. We know the pain, we see it, we feel it. They are the only innocent ones; we, the parents, are the cause of their grief. The blame game divorced people play only drives the knife deeper into their little bleeding hearts.

I prayed, "God forgive us and come with healing in Your wings. You created each one of our children and knew every day of their lives before they left their mother's womb. You knew these days of pain would come into the lives of the innocent. There is no way to make it all right; only You, their Creator and the Healer can bring good out of their places of pain. You, God, are the only perfect parent and all others have failed. You, God, are the only perfect love. You, God, are the only One that can come to their hearts with healing in Your wings and restore the broken places that only You can see. I pray today for wisdom for days ahead, that we might parent with Your love and grace and mercy. Draw us all closer to You and closer to one another as the years go by and for this I will forever be grateful."

There was a stirring down the dark hallway; I heard little girls talking and laughing together in their double bed.

Yes, it was Thanksgiving Day! In just a few hours, there would be turkey, mashed potatoes and gravy, dressing, peas, deviled eggs, cranberry sauce and maybe a new cabbage casserole, then pecan and pumpkin pie for desert! Football games and naps on the couch, late-night turkey sandwiches on not-so-healthy white bread. This was the beginning of a new family ... new traditions, new experiences and new loves.

We were all living life together, not in Plan A but in Plan B with God's help—Plan B can be a beautiful thing!

I rubbed my eyes and felt myself in my warm bed with my comforter snuggled up under my chin.

A memory from long ago lingered in my mind and lulled me back to sleep. My alarm went off; I slipped my feet out of the warm bed and into my slippers. The house was cool as I made my way to the kitchen to make my coffee and spend time with the Lord before I jumped into holiday preparation mode! And how I loved it! My family was coming to dinner!

Today is Thanksgiving Day 24 years later! The house will soon be full of our adult kids with 11 of our 13 grandchildren running everywhere, ranging from age 15 to our newest 7-month-old bundle of joy!

It will be CRAZY! Our house is still not large enough for everyone. The laughter and teasing keeps everyone moving around, catching up with one another. Cousins meeting new cousins and reminiscing of days gone by. Kids dragging out toys from the laundry room that granny always keep for her little precious ones! I think there must be at least 200 Matchbox cars that have definitely seen better days but they are always a favorite for the little boys. The little girls run for the dress-up box with plastic high heels and doll babies. And then there is always the mad dash for who gets to ride on the little red plastic fire engine with its screaming siren. The older kids will crowd around the couch and pull out their electronic gadgets, laughing at granny who can hardly use her cell phone! Football games on our big-screen TV, always buzzing in the background! The kitchen counter will be filled with turkey and ham and the potluck of assorted sides and yes, even that special cabbage casserole that became a favorite of the Plan B family!

We've been through so much since that first Plan B family Thanksgiving. We've had lots of fun and happy memories but also our share of pain and struggle, but always with the constant grace of the restoring God, working His love into our lives. And we really do love one another! The closed doors opened, and we always found our way back to each other, and a deep love was birthed between us all!

I can hardly think about these people I love so much without tears in my eyes. I don't deserve such a gift of grace, but I am forever thankful for these crazy, beautiful people I call my Plan B family!

God is good! I am one thankful wife and mother and granny! My heart is full!

Happy Thanksgiving! Now, let's pray and eat!

"I praise You for I am fearfully and wonderfully made. Wonderful are Your works; my soul knows it very well. My frame was not hidden from You, when I was being made in secret, intricately woven in the depths of the earth. Your eyes saw my unformed substance; in Your book were written every one of them, the days that were formed for me, when as yet there was none of them. How precious to me are Your thoughts, O God. How vast is the sum of them, if I would count them they are more than the sand; I awake and I am still with You" (Psalm 139:14-18).

"The steadfast love of the LORD never ceases; His mercies never come to an end; they are new every morning; great is Your faithfulness. The LORD is my portion says my soul, therefore I will hope in Him" (Lamentations 3:22-24).

"We love because He first loved us" (1 John 4:19).

"Nothing will be able to separate us from the love of God, that is revealed in Christ Jesus our Lord" (Romans 8:38b).

36
Life with a Bang!

HOT, SALTY AIR, sizzling hamburgers, hickory-flavored smoke, the musty smell of sparklers and laughter … lots of laughter!

That's my memory of the Fourth of July!

As far back as I can remember, my kids have celebrated the Fourth of July at my big brother and his wife's house, their Uncle Sonny and Aunt Polly. They have a big rambling house snuggled in a little cove on the beautiful waters of Grande Lagoon in our hometown. Most families try to get together at Christmas or Thanksgiving, but not ours—we do the Fourth of July! And with a bang I might add!

My sister-in-law Polly was always the hostess with the mostest! Preparing days in advance, she had to have everything just right! From red, white and blue paper plates to American flag napkins, silverware and cups, all matched the motif! The house was decorated everywhere with little American flags! She had prepared every detail of the celebration for our family, even a freezer full of ice-cream sandwiches and cases of sparklers for all the kids later that night!

The cousins started rolling in the week before from all

across the United States, looking forward to lots of home cooking, fishing, swimming, water skiing and pouring over Aunt
Polly's famous scrapbooks, with pictures galore capturing
family memories. There were hours of entertainment spent re-
viewing pictures of days gone by, laughing at each other with
comments: "Remember when we did this?" Kids making fun of
each other and just sharing the love!

Yes, and laughter … lots of laughter!

Finally, the whole gang would be complete and the house
would be infiltrated with kid paraphernalia. Barbie dolls belonging to sweet little girls and the size-15 tennis shoes and
dirty socks of big teenage boys would be scattered everywhere!
Water guns fights, watermelon seed spitting contests and
40-year-olds acting like they were 12 again.

And laughter … lots of laughter!

The big day would stretch on with eating, eating and more
eating, only to be topped by taking pictures, pictures and more
pictures … at every angle, with each family grouping … just
one more shot! Would it ever end with Aunt Polly's picture taking? She would just laugh and tell us we would be glad one
day! We are!

Finally, the day would turn to dusk and the kids would begin to quiet down. Relaxing in lawn chairs spread out beneath
the clear Florida sky, we would watch the sun set over the water. Enjoying just being with family, we would visit with one another and wait for the skies to darken as we settled down for the
grand finale of the day, Uncle Sonny's famous fireworks show!

Sparklers would be opened by the case! Moms would
be watching little hands and feet with shouts of "Be careful,

watch out, and don't burn yourself!" Kids with flaming spar-
kler torches would be running through the yard, writing their
names across the dark sky, and big white 5-gallon buckets of
cold water would eventually be filled with their dead magical
wands! And yes, laughter … lots of laughter!

The biggest kids would be on the beach, across the street,
strategically setting up the grand finale fireworks production.
Did I happen to mention the age of those kids? I guess late 60s
just ensures you have mastered the fine art of the Fourth of July
fireworks spec-tac-u-lar! And a masterpiece it would be! Get
ready … get set … go! Flames would shoot high in the sky, bottle rockets and shooting stars! There would be oohs and aahs
and breathtaking shrills as we watched the dark sky fill with
magical lights! Then it would be over … smoke lingering in the
dark sky and sounds again … of laughter!

The air would be thick and musty with dead bottle rockets
and smoldering sparklers. Dragging lawn chairs back in and
picking up any trash on the lawn, cousins would laugh, little
ones would rub their eyes with sleepy lids and the day would
be over. Another family Fourth of July put to rest!

I love holidays spent with family. I appreciate the fact that
my parents loved all the holidays, and I have many wonderful
holiday family traditions to relive in my mind and pass down to
future generations. But as much as my parents loved their family and enjoyed life, they taught me there was a proper order
of important things. We must love God first, then spouse, then
children and other family members, then church and friends
and all others. My mother made sure I knew that God's love
even included loving our enemies. My parents led by example,

and they loved well.

I haven't always lived like that. It's easy to get our loves out of order and it can cause such damage in our lives. Unless God is FIRST, we will long for our satisfaction and fulfillment in the other loves. They can't take the place within our hearts that can only be filled with God. It's a dangerous thing to call a person your "heart"!

I'm grateful for parents that set the example of priorities for me, even when all I wanted was sparklers and fireworks on the Fourth of July, turkey and dressing at Thanksgiving and presents and candy at Christmastime! Holidays were all about ME having fun! My parents were always pointing me to the deeper meaning of everything, always pointing me to the center of it all … God. Everything else is just a spoke in the wheel of our life as we move through our journey here on earth. Memories can last a lifetime. They are captured in scrapbooks and they remain in our thoughts, but mostly they stay within our hearts.

But truth, well, that's another story. Truth is eternal.

"Jesus answered, 'I am the WAY and the TRUTH and the LIFE. No one comes to the Father except through Me'" (John 14:6).

I'd like to close this with a quote from Jonathan Edwards: "The enjoyment of God is the only happiness with which our souls can be satisfied. To go to heaven fully to enjoy God is infinitely better than the most pleasant accommodations here. These are but shadows, but God is the substance. These are but scattered beams but God is the sun. These are but streams, but God is the ocean."

37
Missing Pieces

SITTING IN A small cubicle, my mother fidgeted with a crumpled napkin. From the corner of my eye I saw her smoothing the paper, then meticulously folding it over and over into smaller squares.

I patted her hand and smiled at her. She smiled back and settled down, just holding the small square parcel of a napkin in her lap.

My mother was in the middle stages of Alzheimer's, and it was our day out together for lunch and a few errands.

We were fortunate to still be able to get out once in a while, but I noticed that she was becoming more and more restless during these ventures. I wondered when it would come to an end ... when we would no longer enjoy these times together.

I moved back to Florida from Colorado when I was in my 20s and lived very close to my mother for most of my adult life. During that time, my mother and I enjoyed many lunches out! She loved to pick up the phone and say, "Get the kids and let's go out to lunch today ... my treat." And we did! But on that day I realized this pleasure was coming to an end.

But ... NOT that day!

On that day we visited her home church, Warrington Presbyterian, where she and my father were charter members. They were planning for their 50th anniversary photo directory. Earlier that month I had taken her to Olan Mills Photographers to have pictures made and it was the day we were to view the photos and choose the one she wanted in the directory.

A young attractive woman entered the small cubicle and sat down. There was a computer screen sitting there facing us with a bright-blue screen saver waving in motions. With some polite introductions out of the way, she brought up the first picture of my mother on the screen before us.

She looked wonderful to me. Her bright-aqua-blue suit, her graying hair with soft waves framing her sweet face, her fading brown eyes behind her glasses, her tilted smile glistening with the lipstick I had dabbed on her before they took the picture … all of it made me smile. I loved her. She was old and feeble and losing her mind, but she was still my mother and she was still the most beautiful woman in the world to me.

Our young saleswoman flashed a few other poses across the screen and then paused and asked which one we liked the most. I looked at my mother and said, "I like the first one the best, which one do you like?"

She turned to me with a very serious look on her face and said, "Who is that old woman?"

I reached over to pat her hand and tried to explain where we were and why, and that the picture on the screen was her. Abruptly, she looked at me, straight in the eye, and forcefully said, "That old woman is NOT me, and I don't know who she is!"

She looked down into her lap and started fumbling with her small napkin, folding and refolding it again.

The Bible tells us plainly, "All flesh is grass, and all its beauty is like the flower of the field. The grass withers, the flower fades, when the breath of the Lord blows upon it; surely the people are grass. The grass withers, the flower fades, but the Word of our God will stand forever" (Isaiah 40:7-8).

I looked at that computer screen filled with the picture of my precious mother and I knew there were pieces missing of her. Oh, she still looked like my beautiful, godly mother ... but she was fading and those parts of her would be forever gone. Those fingers that folded clothes for me and put Band-Aids on my boo-boos were now fumbling with tiny scraps of paper. Sometimes it was too much for me, seeing her fade away—like losing puzzle pieces of a beautiful picture that can't ever be replaced. I loved her so much!

But I love many things!

I love the early break of dawn and its sunrise, crystal blue skies with fluffy white clouds, colorful wildflowers on the side of the road, little tadpoles in our birdbath, tiny hummingbirds in my backyard, the brilliant colors of a slow-setting sun as it disappears beyond the horizon. I just love looking at beautiful sights each day ... gifts of God ... displays of His beautiful handiwork. But just as each of these masterpieces only last for a short time, they change, they disappear, never to return the same way ... each beautiful in its own way, in its own time.

I looked at my own fading mother with the same appreciation and awe of the beauty I see in the sunset ... all pointing me to the same Creator God, the controller and sustainer of all life.

As often as I can be, I am intentional about noticing the beautiful things of God. To be in a place of beauty and actually "see it" allows me to change and behold something much greater than myself. Beauty moves me into a place of awe, and awe erupts within my heart into the explosion of praise to the God of all creation ... from whom all blessings flow. The Bible tells me that He inhabits the praises of His people. As praise begins in my heart and then leaves my mouth, His JOY erupts, filling me, moving me deeper into the knowledge of the love of God, greater than I knew yesterday, last week, last year.

"And this is life eternal, that they may know You, the only true God, and Jesus Christ whom You have sent" (John 17:3).

"Praise the Lord! For it is good to sing praises to our God, He is gracious and lovely; praise is becoming and appropriate" (Psalm 147:1).

"For I am persuaded that neither death, nor life, nor angels, nor principalities, nor things present nor things to come, nor powers, nor height, nor depth, (nor Alzheimer's), nor any other creature, shall be able to separate us from the love of God, which is IN Christ Jesus our Lord" (Romans 8:38-39).

"The Lord takes pleasure in those who reverently and worshipfully fear Him, in those who hope in His mercy and loving-kindness" (Psalm 147:11).

"Shout joyfully to the Lord, all the earth; Break forth in song, rejoice, and sing praises" (Psalm 98:4-5).

My mother was always singing, always praising the Lord, and always trusting in His amazing grace! She loved the Bible.

She trusted what it said. She was now living out what Isaiah 40 said: "Like the grass and the flower … fading away … then one day, she would be gone from this world."

On that day I could see that happening right before my eyes … she was fading away.

I knew that behind the blank face of Alzheimer's, there lived my real mother and she knew that Christ in her was her only hope of glory, and that was enough! Today, her eyes did not recognize her own face on a computer screen but that didn't matter because the Good Shepherd knows His sheep. He is faithful to care for His own all the way home.

I knew that one day she would be gone. She was fine with that. She was longing to be united to THE love of her life. She was not longing to be with her family members who had passed on, or her husband of almost 50 years, although that would happen in heaven. I knew, without a shadow of doubt, her longing was for the Lord.

"Oh, magnify the Lord with me, and let us exalt His name together" (Psalm 34:3).

I finished filling out the order form and picked the first picture that I liked.

She was fumbling again with her little scrap of a napkin. Gently I took her by the hand, the napkin dropped to the floor, and we began making our way out of the church. Timidly, walking very close to me, she tightly held on to my hand, her eyes fixed on me in an almost childlike way. I'm sure I must have done the same to her when I was her little girl.

Everything changes as time goes by ... everything except God! And His Word!

"My soul magnifies the Lord, and my spirit rejoices in God, my Savior" (Luke 1:46-47).

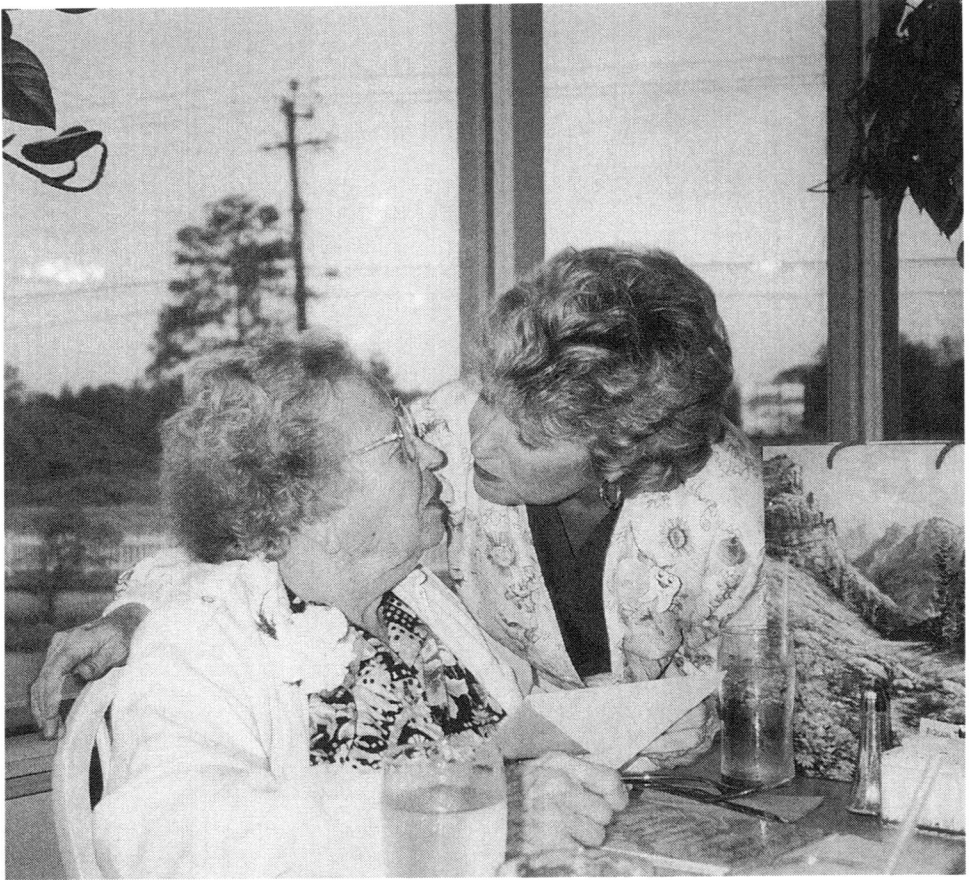

38
Paper Plates and Simple Faith

SITTING QUIETLY WITH her hands folded neatly and resting on the white plastic table in the fellowship hall at her church was my little mother.

Kind faces leaning over her, some with hugs and occasionally a kiss on her cheek, the people came to our table in droves.

She was clueless.

She had Alzheimer's.

My mother lived in an elderly care facility and this was our day out to celebrate the anniversary of Warrington Presbyterian Church. My parents had been charter members. They were not only charter members, but my father had been an elder and my mother a Sunday school teacher, Bible school teacher, nursery worker, kitchen helper, women's Bible study teacher, prayer warrior and probably a helper of whatever kind was needed at the time. They lived at church—their friends were from church, their social life was at church and today, she was clueless.

We sat down at a long table in the fellowship hall. She was quiet as the pastor began to rehearse the history of the church and to thank those who had started the work. My parents were honored—my mother never even blinked when they mentioned my parents' names. I smiled at her and she smiled back. Thankfully she still recognized me.

A blessing for the food was given. I patted her hand and told her to stay right there and I would get her something to eat. I placed a few tablespoons of her favorite foods on her paper plate. My mother always ate in moderation just like she had lived her life. Her baby daughter, though, was another story altogether. Trying to pile all the things I loved on my little paper plate while balancing my mother's plate was a challenge. But I was up for it! Fried chicken, potato salad, collard greens and then banana pudding … I carefully made my way back to the table. She smiled at me with my big plate of food. Years ago she would have made a comment but that day she just smiled. She sat there quietly, like a good little girl, and began to eat.

The down-home country food was delicious! You just can't beat dinner on the grounds in an old southern church! We both thoroughly enjoyed it and then it started.

There was a rumble of voices, people seeing others they had not seen in years, finally making the connection of who was who after all those years! Laughter and kisses and hugs were everywhere!

People in their 50s and 60s began coming over to our table. "Mrs. Burge, I want to thank you so much for all you taught me while I was here. I was stationed at the naval air station, going to school for a while and since this church was so close to the base, I attended here and was in your Sunday school class. You taught me to love God's Word and to pray, and my life took on a whole new meaning after being here in Pensacola." They would go on to tell her about their family, what they had done in their life since then and to thank her profusely, and then another would take their place.

And again, she was clueless.

I wasn't clueless — I was crying.

Of course, I wished my mother could enjoy those people from her past but that's really not why I was crying. I wasn't sad. I had come to accept where she was. Her three children had become her parents. We accepted the loss of the mother we once knew. We were dealing with it as best we knew how. We loved her. She was the weak one now and we had to make the decisions for her. Alzheimer's is sad and the losses are many. But that is not why I cried …

I cried because it was beautiful.

A life lived in the ordinary — in humility, simplicity and unselfishness — loving God, His Word and serving others. And the fruit of her life was flourishing even though the life of the servant was ebbing away.

There was this same overlying comment from most of the people who stopped by our table. She had such an infectious love for the Lord, His Word, the Bible and prayer, they followed her path!

I leaned over the table and picked up my mother's Bible and smiled. Years of use, it was all underlined in red and the pages worn thin. She couldn't read it anymore, but she liked to hold it. I often thought she almost held it like a little child, a soft security blanket. She still knew somehow she needed it … it gave her comfort.

After the line thinned from so many people stopping by to talk to my mother, she looked at me with a confused look and asked, "Who are all these people anyway? I want to go home!" I chuckled … she smiled … oblivious again.

Alzheimer's patients don't really do well with change, and she was in a strange place. She just wanted to go back home where she felt safe and more comfortable.

I took her by the hand, we deposited our paper plates into the large trash can by the exit and left the church where she had spent her life to go back to the square little room at the nursing home where she felt safe.

My mother is gone now, but I think of her often. Her simple unassuming ways. Her life was lived in the ordinary, and yet she was content and even joyful as she loved and served others selflessly. She never, ever wanted to be in the spotlight!

I am soooo NOT like her. She never once worked outside the home. I did for more than 30 years. She never once colored her hair. I can't remember when I didn't. She always wore simple, modest clothes. The brighter and more bling for me, the better. She lived in moderation. When I like something, I have a very hard time stopping at one! She never wanted to be in the spotlight. I was born enjoying it.

I am crying now … missing her.

Even though we are not alike on so many levels, she did "infect" me, like so many others through the years, infected with seeking the Lord for the indescribable joy of His presence.

I saw that day, in the church fellowship hall, with the people from my mother's past, that her seeking and seeing God in His Holy Word was tantalizing for others as well on the same path.

Her light radiated with God so others could see the way to go. She was just a little ahead on the path of joy. But that day in the fellowship hall, I saw the beauty of it all—her devoted life had left a trail of Jesus followers. She had pointed to His glory and that day, once again, she was clueless, unaware of all the praise she was receiving.

And that is the way she would have wanted it, because her life was all about the glory of God, not the exaltation of Jo Burge!

Her journey had reached a stopping point at the door of Alzheimer's. She would never walk away from it and be the mother I once knew, but she did eventually go through it. I know she was greeted on the other side by the One she had loved for so long.

"And his master said to him, 'Well done, good and faithful servant. You were faithful with a few things. I will put you in charge of many things. Enter into the joy of the Lord'" (Matthew 24:21).

"Who shall separate us from the love of Christ? Shall tribulation or distress or persecution or famine or nakedness or peril or sword? Just as it is written, 'For Thy sake we are being put to death all day long; we were considered as sheep to be slaughtered.' But in ALL these things we overwhelmingly conquer through Him who loved us. For I am convinced that neither death, nor life, nor angles, nor principalities, nor things present, nor things to come, nor powers, nor height, nor depth, nor any other created thing, (nor Alzheimer's), shall be able to separate us from the love of God which is IN Christ Jesus our Lord" (Romans 8:35-39).

"For I am the Lord, that is my name; I will not give My glory to

another" (Isaiah 42:8).

"But as for me, I trust in Thee O Lord, I say, Thou art my God, my times are in His hand" (Psalm 30:14).

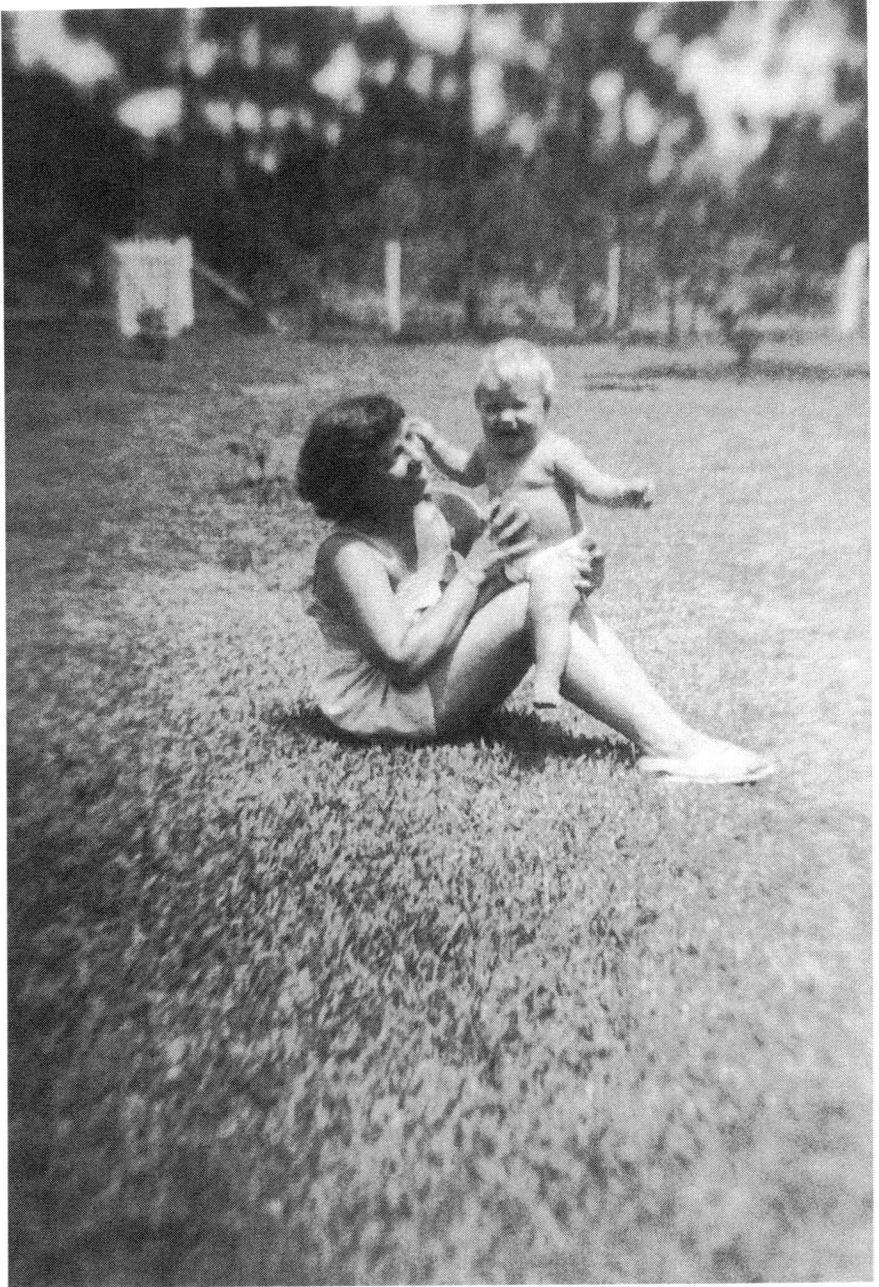

39
Mama's Baby

IT WAS A bleak and cloudy day in February. I had just returned from attending a funeral of an elderly woman in our church.

I go to a lot of funerals since my husband is a minister. Each time I sit and listen to him preach and rehearse the message of the brevity of human life, I drift away into my own thoughts … of life and death and the importance of knowing the love of God, the love of family and holding on to cherished memories.

That day the funeral was especially emotional for me as it had been almost one year since I was the one sitting at the front of the church, along with the other members of my family, staring at a delicate pink casket containing the lifeless shell of my precious little mother.

I rejoice today knowing that my mother is with the Lord and filled with joy beyond measure, but this year has been hard for me—I have missed her terribly. Reliving memories of ordinary days and growing up in Beach Haven has comforted me.

I was my mother's baby. I guess if you are the youngest in the family, no matter how old you become, you will always be "mama's baby." Many times this year I have wished I could be her baby just one more day, crawl up into her comfortable lap, hear her sing to me and feel her soft hands rubbing my back and whispering to me, "Thea, everything's going to be alright."

In 1949 when my mother found out she was pregnant with me, she was not thrilled! She already had a 17-year-old son and a 10-year-old daughter. Baby days were over and so having a baby at almost 40, especially during those hard times after the war, was not something she looked forward to.

I was told later that when she found out she was pregnant, she went into hysterics at the thought of how they could survive. My Aunt Cline, her older sister, had to slap her to stop her uncontrollable crying. She reminded her that "God would get her through it … that I might be the child of her travail but the child of great promise." My mother used to tell me that story, but as a child I never could understand what she meant.

I remember her hands. They were plain, soft hands with clean nails, cut very short, with a simple, ordinary silver wedding band on her third finger of her left hand. They were always smooth and soft, although I knew she was a hard worker. Her veins on the top of her hands reminded me of a road map. I liked to hold her hands and feel the softness. I liked to sit in church and twirl her ring … round and round her finger.

I remember old open-toe black shoes with stubby heels. Those were her Sunday shoes. I loved to put them on and walk around and play dress-up! I loved to live in make-believe, where I was the princess of the world! Her old shoes seemed magical when I slipped my little chubby feet inside. Year after year she wore those shoes. I later noticed they were lined with newspaper—I always wondered why, not realizing that the newspaper lining her shoes meant that each year I would get a new pair of church shoes.

I remember bobby pins and sitting on a little red step ladder in our kitchen on Saturday mornings. She would roll my sun-streaked blonde hair in tiny little circles and pin them to my head. They always reminded me of curly little pigtails covering my chubby round face. She told me I was beautiful … I believed her.

I remember creamy grits when I was sick and the smell of Vicks and warm handkerchiefs tied around my neck. I remember her voice singing to me in the middle of the night when I was scared because I couldn't breathe, sick with the croup I suffered from often as a young child.

I remember long days of hot summer sun and salty water and playing on the beach while my mama, Ms. Thelma and Ms. Susie sat on an old log by the shore, laughing and watching all their children play. They were best friends at a time when you really needed someone close to have as a friend. None of them worked outside the home. Everyone was broke, there was no TV to entertain the kids, and Ms. Thelma did not even have a telephone! Their close friendship helped them keep their sanity during those hard times in which they lived. They were hilarious together! I remember hearing them laugh at silly stories between scoldings for us: "be nice," "share" and "don't go out too far."

I remember bread jugging for minnows and building elaborate sandcastles that were eventually swallowed up by the incoming tide. Hot and tired with our little bodies getting probably way too much sun, we gathered up empty Kool-Aid jugs and wet towels and began to make our way back home. Running through the Browns' yard, then zig-zagging up our red clay road to the end of Colbert Avenue where I lived … I was content. Tomorrow would bring another day of sun and playing with my friends with a fresh palate of white sand for us to build our castles we were all going to live in when we grew up.

I remember the sting of bridal wreath switches and my mother's voice telling me it hurt her more than it hurt me. I never understood how that could be!

I remember story time with my mother when I went to bed at night. Little Golden Books like *The Little Engine That Could, Goosey Loosey and Henny Penny* and *Brer Rabbit*. I remember her singing family ditties and then sweet lullabies like "God Will Take Care of You" and "Safe Am I" as I would drift off to sleep.

I remember my mother standing at the sink washing dishes, singing with my sister and me. Rounds and rounds of Army songs my sister had learned from my older brother about Betty Grable, whoever THAT was! Hymns and hymns and more hymns. Learning to sing alto on "At Calvary." Washing dishes, sweeping the floor, drying dishes and putting them away! My mother NEVER went to bed with dishes in the sink! I never understood that until I had my own kitchen!

I remember the smell of freshly brewed coffee and the aroma of cinnamon-oatmeal cookies. I remember the neighbor ladies coming over to our house around 9 o'clock each morning for coffee and a cookie. Just a short visit but over the years, my mother loved them, prayed for them and provided a safe haven for them to share their deepest concerns. She was like a mother to them, and they loved one another.

I remember years and years of times I would like NOT to remember, when I was living up to my destiny to be the child of travail. The picture of seeing my little mother kneeling beside her bed crying and moaning in agony over my sinful life, carrying me to her Lord, is almost more than I can bear at times. I am forever grateful for her faithfulness to pray for me.

I remember her helping hands when my children were small. I remember how they built forts in her living room with sheets and blankets and then how she crawled inside and had cookies and milk with them. She always kept an imagination basket in her dining room. She saved anything that she thought they could use to create something! Empty containers from concentrated orange juice, milk cartons or the meat trays from the grocery store. There was always colored paper, crayons, scissors and paste, rolled-up newspapers and tape. These treasures provided my children with hours of fun and make-believe!

I remember when she would come over just to fold clothes when I was drowning in laundry. I remember pop-in visits with a casserole and a $20 bill stuck in my pocket when she thought things might be tight in our household. I remember encouraging cards in the mail pointing me to the Lord and His Word. I remember she never involved herself too much in the details of my "drama" of a life. She just prayed for me and loved me unconditionally, pointing me always to the Bible to find the answers I so desperately needed.

I remember the sadness I felt as her mind began to drift away into Alzheimer's and the mother I once knew was no more. Her children became her parents, and we had to make decisions for her. I remember the acceptance we had to face, the letting go and the grace of God that kept her sweet and humble even as she slowly lost the sharp mind she once had. I remember the witness of the constant overflow of gratefulness and appreciation to everyone as she said thank you hundreds of times each day as others cared for her needs. She was an easy woman to love, even as she lost her abilities.

I remember her tired eyes, glazed over with cataracts that would light up as I came into the room. She would point her finger at me, cock her head slightly and say with a big smile, "There she is!" She may not have remembered my name that day, but she knew who I was ... knowing I was hers and she was mine!

I remember the last time I saw that smile. It was minutes away from her death. She died in my arms. I believe that is one of the greatest gifts of grace the Lord has given me ... to hold my little mother while she slipped away from this world into the arms of her Savior. Singing to her the same songs she sang to me: "God Will Take Care of You" and "Safe Am I in the Hollow of His Hands."

"Charm is deceitful and beauty is passing, but a woman who fears the Lord, she shall be praised. Give her the fruit of her hands, and let her own works praise her in the gates" (Proverbs 31:30-31).

"For God so loved the world that He gave His only begotten Son, that whoever believes in Him should not perish but have everlasting life. For God did not send His Son into the world to condemn the world but that the world through Him might be saved. He who believes in Him is not condemned, but he who does not believe is condemned already, because he has not believed in the name of the only begotten Son of God" (John 3:16-18).

40
Whining Wives and Broken Buggies

THERE IS NOTHING as frustrating as trying to grocery shop with a broken buggy! You know, the kind with one wheel lightly chipped? It looks like all the rest, but there is a slight nick in one of its wheels. It's like THAT WHEEL has a mind of its own and it's constantly pulling you to one side or the other. You want to go right, and the broken wheel pulls left. Very irritating! Very frustrating!

Wheels and grocery carts … memories from the past.

I remember going grocery shopping with my mother when I was a child. It was very exciting to a young child during the 1940s.

My parents were middle class, but that meant you didn't have much. I guess we were poor by today's standards, but I did not know that. We had a roof over our head, food on the table, clean clothes to wear and my father had a job. Life was good for me. Of course, there was never any extra money, no air conditioning, no television, no special outings, but I didn't know any difference. That's just the way life was for me, and I was fine with it. It was normal. I was happy and did not need anything else.

My life was pretty much spent at home, playing in the woods nearby or on the beach near our house. When not at home, I was either at school or church. That was pretty much it! We lived simply. We did not go out and eat in restaurants or take vacations, except maybe to go and visit a relative once in a while.

But there was a special occasion during each month that I remember well. I looked forward to it with much anticipation: going to the grocery store early on Saturday morning with my mother!

We only had one car that my father used for work each day, so grocery shopping was done on a Saturday morning after my father's payday. I was thrilled with the thought!

Saturday morning came and after eating breakfast together, reading a Bible verse and saying our morning prayer, we were off to do our chores. I made my bed, straightened my room, got dressed, brushed my teeth and then ran outside to play on my rope swing that hung from the tall pine tree in our front yard. Many times my mother would also take our neighbor, Mrs. Brown, affectionately referred to as Ms. Thelma. Ms. Thelma did not drive. She had seven children and was always very busy, but she and my mother were best friends. They shopped together on Saturday mornings. They were absolutely hilarious together, and it was really fun to go with them.

I was given a very special job to do at the grocery store. I was the one who would get to pick out the buggy for my mother. I would jump out of the car, run into the store where all the buggies were lined up in rows and then pick just the right one for us to use. I would drive it over to my mother, then hang on the front as she drove it up and down the aisles, filling it up with groceries for the next few weeks.

But sometimes, in my excitement, I would grab a broken buggy! They all looked alike, but they weren't!

Nothing is more irritating to a busy mother shopping for groceries with a young child hanging on the front end than to try and drive straight with a broken wheel! It's constantly pulling you in the opposite direction. Frustrating …

This morning in my quiet time with the Lord, I read from the book of Hebrews: "Obey your leaders and submit to them, for they keep watch over your souls, as those who will give an account. Let them do this with JOY and not with grief for that would be unprofitable for you."

Obey, submit, give an account with joy … words women don't like to hear so much in the times we live today, but there they are, in God's Word, the Bible. Black-and-white pages of printed words with the voice of God speaking to my heart.

I stop awhile and think of those words and the responsibility given by God to my husband, an imperfect man given a responsibility from God to lead, to watch out for my soul. He is the one God has called to lead me, to lead our family. One day he will have to give God an account of those he has been called to lead, just like the Bible says. I think about those words as I look into my own heart. On his day of account, what will he say about me? Will he be able to say I was a joy to lead or will he have to say that I was always pulling another way, trying to manipulate and get my own way? Will he say I was a frustration to him as he led me?

I prayed, "Oh, God, help me, I don't want my life to be like a broken buggy! I don't want to be frustrating to him! Create in me, O God, a sweet and gentle spirit which is precious in Your sight."

And that, dear ones, is truly a miracle from God!

But I believe in miracles!

41
Daybreak

SOUND ASLEEP IN my comfortable bed, soft pillows under head, my down comforter pulled snug under my chin, consciousness rolls in like the mist over the bayou.

I begin to wake.

Drifting in and out of consciousness, I sense a loving presence, a quiet voice in my head speaking tenderly to me. Words of a hymn or part of a scripture verse tap on my mind. Sometimes it's just a feeling of warmth or peace or safety, but I feel it and it rouses me from my slumber.

I remember where I am … in a lovely home, safe in a soft warm bed, lying next to the man I love and who loves me. I hear his breathing next to me and I thank God. He is a good man, and I am a blessed woman. I begin thanking God. There is still a sleepy peacefulness as I lay there and slowly break through to full consciousness and then it happens!

As sure as the sun comes up each day, it comes to me, crashing into my mind like a freight train … darkness! Fear, worry, pride, critical thoughts of others. I hate these thoughts but they come to me each morning—haunting me, hounding me, reminding me of reality. I don't have what it takes, nor do those

I love. Dark thoughts tighten their grip on me, desiring to crush me. Why, after all these years, do they still come? Where do they come from?

But I also hear His voice: "Thea, come to Me. I have something for you. I will calm the fears, remove the worry, heal you and fill you with love so you can love others and release them to Me. They will never give you what you truly need. Come to Me."

Quickly I get up and begin to move toward the voice. I rise from my bed and begin my morning routine. It may be 3:30 or 5:30, but it's always early and it's always the same routine.

I walk to the bathroom thanking God for my legs, my feet, my hands, the air I breathe, the warm water to wash my face. I drink a small glass of apple cider vinegar water as I move to the kitchen and make a pot of coffee. I exercise all my joints while I wait for the coffee to brew.

Finally, I kneel down and place my forehead on the floor and speak, "Have mercy on me, O God, a sinner. I am yours, your bondslave, be it unto me, according to Your Word." I continue to bow down and praise Him, saying, "Bless the Lord, O my soul, and all that is within me. Bless His Holy Name, and do not forget all His benefits. He forgives all my iniquities. He heals all your diseases. He redeems your life from destruction and crowns you with loving kindness and tender mercies; for in these, He delights. He fills your mouth with good things and renews your strength like the eagles. Bless the Lord, O my soul, and all that is within me. Bless His Holy Name" (Luke 18:13b, 1:38b; Psalm 103:1-5, 119:50, 16:11, 118:24).

I say the Lord's Prayer each day on my knees. I move to my chair, the private place I meet with God each day. I start singing first, usually "Holy, Holy, Holy" or "Amazing Grace" or "Great Is Thy Faithfulness." Gathering my Bible and prayer books, I come to Him, my mind still swimming with the dark and all too familiar thoughts. They run after my mind like a starving dog, a bloody piece of meat, until I throw myself into His Holy Word. I open the pages desperately seeking relief, wanting to see Him, needing Him to fill the parched and dry places of my soul.

I often find myself crying. I read and see Him coming to me. I hear His voice whispering to me as I read His words, calming me, cleansing me, filling me with the truth of who He is. Waves of joy begin to spring up inside me, shattering the darkness like empty bubbles, ushering me into the secret place of joy in His presence.

"Oh how I love Your Word, it is my comfort in my affliction. At Your right hand there is pleasure forevermore. Yes, I can live again, another day. I can be glad again, another day. I can love again, another day. Yes, this is the day the Lord has made, and I will rejoice and be glad in it!"

I have been meeting early with God in His Word for over 35 years and yet it is still the same each morning. I am reminded every day I wake that I am a great sinner—pride, selfishness, fear, worry, all knocking at the door of my mind seeking entrance. His Word tells me that I must rule over it, but I know I can't do it within myself. But I don't have to; I have a Savior who is greater than my sin. My thoughts are fleeting. His Word … eternal.

I am pressed toward the God who has pressed me into the bosom of Christ. Often I close my quiet time by singing to myself a song my mother sang to me as a little girl:

"Safe Am I"

Safe am I, safe am I, in the hallow of His hands. No fear can harm me, no fear alarm me for He keeps both day and night.

Oftentimes, when my mother sang to me, especially in times of sickness, she would put my name in the song. In my memory, I hear her voice singing God's Word to me: "Safe is Thea, safe is Thea, in the hallow of His hands."

"He has not dealt with us according to our sins, nor rewards us according to our iniquities. For as high as the heavens are above the earth so great is His lovingkindness toward those who fear him. As far as the east is from the west, so far He has removed our transgressions from us. Just as a father has compassion on his children so the Lord has compassion on those who fear Him. For He knows our frame He is mindful that we are but dust. But the loving-kindness of the Lord is from everlasting to everlasting on those who fear Him" (Psalm 103:10-14, 17).

"But may all who seek You rejoice and be glad in You; may those who love Your salvation, say continually, 'Great is the LORD!' As for me, I am poor and needy, but the Lord takes thought for me. You are my help and deliverer" (Psalm 40:16-17).

&

THEN THERE WERE
T·H·R·E·E

42
And Then There Were Three

SITTING AT A stoplight on my way to work, I continued the argument I was having with God.

It had been ongoing for a while now. I wanted something and He wasn't giving it to me.

I tried reasoning with Him and using my best persuasion to try to convince Him of the reasons He should give me what I thought was best ... but nothing ... only silence.

On top of that thought, I was also trying to memorize a scripture verse for the Bible study lesson I would be teaching at church.

I'm a preacher's wife.

I'm a very different kind of preacher's wife.

I'm a divorced woman married to a divorced preacher.

That doesn't happen very often in the Bible Belt where we live.

We were both previously married for a very long time. My husband for 19 years and me for 23 years. A whole other life-time! Neither of us desired to be divorced, but we are. We both have children who have been negatively affected by divorce, as all children who have had that wound forced upon them. Yes, we are labeled a dysfunctional family.

But we both belong to Christ, and He has not rewarded us according to our own iniquities but according to His loving-kindness He has blessed us, in Christ. We were forgiven children and then, by His grace alone, He gave us another mate to share the rest of our lives with. Our marriage is truly a gift to each of us.

But I was totally unprepared to be a preacher's wife! I'm living in a whole new world! I had no clue how to do it, and it is scary at times! I now have five children and a full-time job in a dental office, teach a ladies' Sunday school class and a mid-week ladies' Bible study and go to church every time the door is open and sometimes even late at night with my husband when he has to catch up on something he needs to do behind the scenes. We are "on call" 24 hours a day to help meet the needs of our church family, and as a preacher's wife, I have no really close friends. I am happy in my new life but feeling very, very stretched!

And because of all this, I thought I had a good argument with God for my case!

Preachers' wives don't work full time away from home! My life is just too busy!

In my view, preachers' wives stay home. They head up Bible school in the summertime, teach mid-day Bible studies and cook during the day, and have people over at night. Their houses are neat and picked up, and they never have problems with their kids because mom is at home and the kids are being loved and guided by the preacher's wife and supermom.

I have been in this new marriage several years now and my

life is sooooo NOT like this. It's almost funny!

But it wasn't funny to me that morning. I was stressed … majorly stressed … and on top of that, preachers have to be everyone's friend, so I don't really have anyone I can talk to about the feelings I am having. So I just kept begging God to get on board with my prayer request! "Please, God, let our church pay my husband enough money so I can stay home; then life will be wonderful and I can be a superwife and supermom! Is that too much to ask, Lord? It's not like I want a big car or a fancy house … I just want to stay home and be a full-time wife and mother and serve You, God. I have waited several years and I'm getting a little impatient with You. Are You even listening to me?"

Stopped at the red light, I noticed a 3x5 card taped to my dashboard and remembered, "I'm supposed to be working on remembering this Bible verse."

John 15:5 says, "I am the vine; you are the branches. If you remain in Me and I in you, you will bear much fruit; apart from Me you can do nothing."

I knew that "Jesus is the vine," and I knew that I am "one of His branches" and I DID want to bear much "fruit" for Him in my life; I just thought I knew where and when that would happen, and it wasn't THERE in that situation I found myself in. That WAS the case for my whole argument!

I kept rehearsing those Bible words as I sat there at the red light that early weekday morning. All of a sudden, tears began to well up in my eyes. That inner prompting of the Holy Spirit's voice led me to understand His words of scripture piercing my impatient heart with His words: "Apart from Me, (Thea), you can do nothing! Nothing! NOTHING!"

"Who do I think I am, God?"

"Apart from Him, Thea, you are nothing and you can do nothing!"

The light changed to green and I could hardly see it as the tears rolled down my cheeks. I knew my mascara was going to bleed everywhere.

That word—"nothing"—pierced my heart and brought me, once again, to my knees, even as I sat in my car slowly driving to the dental office where I worked.

During the 2-mile journey, I repented once again of wanting to be the boss of me, the chubby little tan girl rearing her self-willed head!

"Lord, forgive me. I submit to You. I don't know what a preacher's wife is supposed to look like. I don't know what a godly wife or mom is supposed to look like to YOU. Only You know what You want to do IN me and what You want to do THROUGH me and where You want me to BE in order to do that. I let go of my plans of what, where and how YOU will accomplish Your will for my life. I receive whatever lies before me, even if I never get to be home and I have to work outside until I can't work anymore. I say yes to You, Thy will be done!"

Sitting out in the parking lot of my workplace, I dried my tears, reapplied my makeup and put on a happy face! I accepted the loss of my dreams, once again, as being good for me. His touch to me in that car was enough.

His touch is always enough, especially when life is hard! He loves me and I am not alone. He always knows what's best. I can trust Him and let go, especially when life doesn't make sense to me.

That day of surrender was one of many that changed the course of my life. I need to remember it often because the chubby little tan girl forgets and once again tries to be the boss of me!

Not long after that experience at the stoplight, a new dental assistant came to work in our office. Her name was Leslie. She was a very pretty young woman of Filipino/Caucasian heritage.

We did not hit it off. I think most of the girls I worked with thought I was a religious nutcase!

One day while passing through our staff kitchen, I overheard Leslie asking all the girls around the table what they believed about God! Ignoring me, she was asking everyone else! And everyone had an opinion, of course, as everyone does!

Walking past all the girls, going to my office, the Lord prompted me: "You need to start praying for that girl, Leslie."

We weren't really even friends at that time, but I knew the Lord's leading, and so I began to pray for her. I even placed her name on our church prayer list. This went on for more than a year, this praying for the little girl who avoided me.

One midweek morning on a day we did not have patients, I had to run up to the office to pick up something and there was Leslie, in the lab, ordering supplies. We spoke politely, I got what I went in for and then jumped into my car to go about my business.

But NO, the Lord said: "You need to invite Leslie to church tonight."

I ignored Him.

"Thea, you really need to go inside and invite her to church tonight."

I squirmed and answered, "She won't come. She doesn't even

really like me. She never talks to me like she does the other girls."

"That doesn't matter; just do what I'm telling you to do."

Unwillingly, I removed the keys from the ignition, walked right up to Leslie and said, "One of our best friends, who is a missionary, is speaking at our church tonight and I'd like to invite you. Here's the address if you think you might be able to come."

She took the information and politely said, "I'll think about it."

Finally, cranking up the car and driving away, I didn't think she would come. After all, she really didn't even like me.

Sitting in church later that night, I turned around and saw her pretty face as she was walking down the aisle. She sat down right next to me. Little did I know, that night our lives were to be forever changed.

Our friend presented the gospel message and later that night, Leslie received Jesus as her Lord and Savior and was forever united into the family of God. We were to enjoy a long, but at many times "wild and crazy," relationship as mother and daughter in Christ. But I didn't know it at that time.

You see, I didn't really know her and she didn't know me.

But God knew us both and in His sovereign will and timing, He gave US as a gift to one another, a gift of grace that would grow and be fruitful over the years.

We began meeting together after work one night a week to study the Bible and pray. She also started going to our church but our after-work meetings were intimate and became a place of safety and love, healing and growth.

Not long after we began meeting together, another young beautiful woman started working at our dental office. She

shared the dental chair right next to Leslie. Her name was Debbie, and she was a spitfire! She also thought I was a religious
nutcase and avoided me. Walking through the staff kitchen, I
could hear her talk, and she was very opinionated and definitely had her guard up. I surmised she had probably been hurt
in her past, and I prayed for her also. My new little daughter
Leslie also cared about Debbie and asked her one day to come
to our Bible study. Debbie laughed. She DID NOT need Bible
study! Leslie asked, "Well, would you come in and let us at least
pray for you?" Debbie said she had been prayed for before and
nothing had ever happened but, "Oh well, it couldn't hurt."
She walked in, with her heart of stone, fists up, guarding the
wounds deep within, and in a very short conversation about
faith in Christ and a prayer, she was forever changed! God gave
her a new heart to love Him, and the walls of fear and pain began to crumble. We were united in a love that would never die.
I would also come to love her as my own daughter.

And then we were three ...

We continued to meet after work once a week. We read
the Bible, we prayed, we cried and bled with each other and
through Christ, we came to love each other deeply.

I guess it showed because one day, when we were getting
charts for our patients and all of us were talking about our wonderful Lord, I saw another pretty face staring at us. She was also
a new girl in the office, very pretty but quiet. I never heard her
opinions being voiced around the kitchen table. She just appeared
to me, as one standing at a distance, listening to others, wanting
something but not knowing what it was. But there was sadness
in her dark brown eyes. I didn't know her either, but somehow I

felt we shared something—perhaps the pain I saw hidden in her eyes. But that day, when I saw her watching us, straining to hear what we were saying, I began praying for her also.

I can't remember which of us invited beautiful Marisha to our after-work Bible study, but before long, we had three little girls who met with the old woman who didn't want to be working … but was!

Our relationship grew and through the years, there have been many women who came into the old woman's office, for a while, to taste what it felt like to be real and needy and then nourished by God and His Word. We loved each other for a time, and then they moved on, shining their light of Christ in a different workplace.

But the three pretty faces I hold so dear in my heart are forever God's gifts of grace to a stubborn preacher's wife who finally said "Yes, Lord" at the red light. "Thy will be done! I am not the boss of me, You are, God!"

My husband is now a retired preacher, and I no longer work in a dental office. We don't have a house full of kids, and I'm not at church every time the door is open. I now have time to breathe. I can wake up when I want to and go to sleep when I want to. We have been given the privilege to travel and enjoy so much of God's majestic beauty along the way. And we love it!

But daily I still have to do battle with the chubby little tan girl who wants to be the boss of me! Often I have to remind myself of the three JOYS that came into my life when I said no to me and yes to God and His will, when it was NEVER what I wanted but was always His will for the expanse of His kingdom and for His glory! It's never all about me, it's about HIM and His glory! But the really beautiful thing about obedience is that eventually it bears fruit, and often overflowing JOY fruit!

These three women, Leslie, Debbie and Marisha, are the JOY fruit of His glory, given as gifts of His grace to a stubborn preacher's wife who finally gave up! Our lives have parted now, but I still watch them from a distance, and it's beautiful! I see them, still loving the Lord, still loving His Word, still loving others, letting the light of Christ shine through their broken but healed lives, keeping their eye on the prize: Christ in us, our hope of glory!

I pray, "Thank you, Father, for those gifts of grace to me! My daughters and sisters-in-love in Christ!"

(Jesus speaking) "If you remain in Me, and I in you, you will bear fruit; apart from Me, you can do nothing. If you remain in Me and My words remain in you, ask what you wish and it will be done for you. This is to My Father's glory, that you bear much fruit, showing yourselves to be My disciples. As the Father has loved Me, so have I loved you. Now remain in My love. If you keep my commandments, you will remain in My love, just as I have kept my Father's commands and remain in His love. I have told you this so that my JOY may be IN you and that your JOY many be complete. My command is this; Love each other as I have loved you" (John 15:5, 2-8, 9-12).

"Not that I have already obtained this or am already perfect, but I press on to make it my own because Christ Jesus has made me His own. Brothers, I do not consider that I have made it my own. But one thing I do; forgetting what lies behind and straining forward to what lies ahead, I press on toward the goal for the prize of the upward call of God in Christ Jesus" (Philippians 3:12-14).

43
Miracle on a Street Corner at Disney

HEARING MY NAME called out, I rose from my chair and made my way to the front of the room. Turning around I saw an array of different colored faces all smiling at me. I stood out in stark contrast like others who also wore white skin. There were several blacks, assorted hues, but the majority of the faces were brown—not really even brown, but almost like soft, buttery caramel. But they were all smiling! Many big and beautiful smiles with pearly white teeth in contrast to their dark faces. Other smiles were toothless or only sparsely populated, but still smiling all the same.

I smiled back at them with my large mouth, with lots of teeth straightened by my orthodontist when I was a teenager, and introduced myself.

"Hi, my name is Thea Coker, and I live in Pensacola, Florida, in the United States of America. It is my pleasure to be with you today and share my story with you!"

And this is where it all began, the miracle on a street corner at Disney!

I was in the Philippines on a medical/dental mission trip. Mission trips were not new to me as my husband is a pastor and I had been with him many times before, but this time, I was alone.

The plan had been worked on for months by the sponsoring churches and many hours spent in the preparation for the two weeks we would be in the Philippines. There were several different cities where we would set up camp and minister to the nationals, but the bigger picture was always the same. The week before, local Christians walked through the villages passing out notifications that we would be coming to their area and how they could get to our location. There would be doctors, nurses, dentists, pastors and many others to offer support and help, all at no cost to them. Much time had been spent in prayer and preparation for our arrival, as well as the requisitioning of local help, as much as possible, from a very poor population. Our mission crew spent two days sorting through boxes and boxes of free prescription medications and OTC meds and vitamins, which we sorted and repackaged in smaller containers in order to distribute as much as we could to as many people as possible. We were already tired before we even began.

So on that day, it was my turn—I was up!

I was there at center stage for the most important thing: the beautiful, miraculous story of a sinner saved by the grace of the beautiful, miraculous everlasting God of the Bible!

"I'm Thea, and I'd like to tell you my story," my interpreter echoed in Tagalog.

For the next few minutes I unfolded the story of my life. I tried to be transparent in my failures and my desperation for inner peace. I told them of the day that I came to know the Lord in a personal way and the miraculous change He had made within my heart over the years since that time.

The beautifully colored faces in the room were all fixed on me. I noticed a few women softly crying as our eyes connected for a moment and we exchanged loving smiles. I finished my story then sat down on the wooden bench in the front. The pastor began to explain in more detail the experience of personal salvation through Christ and offered prayer and counseling for any who might have questions.

The group was finally dismissed with instructions for where to go for medical or dental treatment.

Suddenly, I was grabbed by a young Filipino woman with a big smile on her face. She kept hugging me and saying, "Mama, mama!"

I did not know what was going on, but would soon find out, as she was to be my interpreter in the dental area. We would work together with the oral surgeon for the rest of our trip.

Her name was Bing. She was an orphan of a Filipino father and an American mother. I looked at the picture she held in her hand and yes, I did resemble her mother. We actually looked like sisters. Bing and I were to become fast friends! By the time I left, I loved her as a daughter, even though I thought we would never set eyes on one another again!

Walking together into the room that had been prepared for dental work, it was daunting to say the least! We were in a classroom of an old broken-down school building. There was no electricity or running water. The large room was set up with chairs leaning against the walls, with 5-gallon buckets with 2 to

3 inches of dirt in the bottom sitting near each chair. There was a large table in the middle of the room with a Coleman stove set up with a big pot of boiling water and dental instruments lying on clean towels next to it. This was it, our dental operatory for the next week and a half. The line outside was long, hundreds of people waiting for us, all with big smiles on their faces. I was so convicted of my own American shallowness.

My new friend Bing began speaking to the native people in Tagalog, explaining to them the process for the day. They would all be seen by a dentist, address their most pressing pain issues and then would be given medications and vitamins as they left.

And so we began.

One after another they came with their smiles for us, so grateful for the hands of a dentist who would take away their pain. My doctor wore a miner's light around his head. I held a flashlight in one hand with my other hand free for instrument assisting. Because there was no electricity for suction, I tried to keep blood flow at a minimum by swabbing with gauze in between his efforts to remove the broken teeth that were causing the most pain for my new, precious Filipino friends.

The big bucket was soon being filled with bloody spit and broken teeth. One after another, my oral surgeon did his magic and relieved these precious people from their dental pain. It was beautiful! We were paid with hugs and gauze-filled mouths stretched with smiles as they rose from the chair with hands full of penicillin and multiple vitamins.

The conditions were horrible: sweltering, dark, dingy and exhausting. There was not much time to talk during the day as we were constantly working. But we took a short lunch break and that's when I came to know my newfound daughter-in-love, Bing.

She had lost both her parents and life had been difficult for her. Everything changed when she became a Christian and now she was a dedicated missionary. Her fiancé was also a missionary who was living up in the mountains working with the pygmies, a very dangerous group of people in the Philippines. Her love for the Lord was so obvious!

We laughed, we talked about our pasts, and we shared our dreams with each other on those daily lunch breaks. We instantly loved each other, even though our time together was short. I think, since I looked so much like her mother, somehow she felt her memory in my love for her.

Being much older than my little Bing, I tried to encourage her in her faith. One of her daydreams was to come to America and get to see Mickey Mouse at Disney World! We laughed! She thought this was a silly dream and told me that this would probably NEVER happen because she was poor. I told her, "Don't give up on your dream. You never know what the Lord has in store for you, and He can do anything!" Yes, she would keep the dream somewhere on a shelf in her heart.

The long days came and went, and it was finally time to leave the Philippines. We hugged, we cried and thanked the Lord for letting us meet. We kissed and promised, "I'll see you in heaven one day, my friend!"

In time I did not think about my little friend Bing.

Life was busy. I was a pastor's wife and also worked full time in a dental office. At times, I felt like my life was one rushing roller coaster! I needed a break to come up for air, and I was going to get one! My doctor was taking our entire staff to the National Orthodontic Convention in Orlando, Florida. We would be there for a week, and he was giving us time off to spend at Disney World for a mini vacation! What a guy … the staff was busy getting ready and anxiously awaiting our free time at Disney World!

Meetings, meetings, more meetings, and then finally the end of the dental convention! Our large office split up into several small groups and made plans of where we wanted to spend our free day. I joined up with several friends and we decided it was the Magic Kingdom for us, where "dreams come true!" We laughed a lot, ate too much and enjoyed ourselves immensely!

Winding down the end of a long day, several of my friends needed to take a potty break and so we stopped at a restaurant and began taking turns in the bathroom.

Miraculously, I didn't need a potty break, so I just hung around outside, standing next to the street post waiting for my friends!

Then I heard it: "Mama, mama!"

I jerked myself around and yes, there she was, my little brown Bing! I couldn't believe it! We hugged and laughed and spun around like we were playing ring-around-the-rosie! How could this be?

As my dental friends gathered around us, they too couldn't believe what had just happened! Meeting Bing, my little precious "love daughter" from the Philippines on a street corner in Disney World!

After we both settled down, she told me that she had been sent to America with a child who needed surgery. It was arranged by the missionaries to send her to America for the surgery at no cost to the little girl. But they needed an interpreter ... my Bing.

The surgery had been successful, and they were giving Bing one day at Disney World before returning home to the Philippines the very next day!

But for that one moment in time, we met, we walked into a magical sphere of God's loving grace, given to each of us that day, a miracle on a street corner in Disney!

So, don't give up on your dreams. Just tuck them away on a shelf in your heart. Look up to Jesus and rest. He knows the best way to put a life together and sprinkle it with HIS magic ... AMAZING GRACE!

"And no creature is hidden from His sight, but all are naked and exposed to the eyes of Him to Whom we must give an account" (Hebrews 4:13).

"You know when I sit down and when I rise up; You discern my thoughts afar. You search out my path and my lying down and are acquainted with all my ways. Even before a word is on my tongue, behold, O LORD, you know it all together" (Psalm 139:2-4 [my favorite Psalm]).

"I know the things that come into your mind, every one of them" (Ezekiel 11:5).

44
Dance of the Wheelchair

I WAS PRAYING: "Lord, you know I don't want to do this."

I felt the anxiety of fear rising in my chest.

Sitting at the end of a long row of chairs in the waiting room of the hospital, there was a woman in a wheelchair. Hands folded in her lap, she just quietly stared ahead. A hospital employee rolled her in and then left her abruptly.

I was there in the waiting room because my husband was in the hospital after a car accident. He was having treatment for severe cellulitis, an infection resulting from an injury. A rupture in his colon had spread infection throughout his body and he almost died. Thankfully, they were able to get it under control, but each day he endured the pain of being lowered into a large tub of water to soak and clean out the wound. Movement of any kind was excruciating. I hated seeing him suffer so I usually stayed in the waiting room and prayed, and that's where I was.

I finished reading a story in an issue of *Guideposts* magazine that inspired me in my walk of faith. I was sitting there meditating on the truths I had just read when they rolled the woman in and left her alone in the corner of the room.

She was African-American, probably in her mid-80s, with

her gray hair braided and pinned to the top of her head. She had a soft, gentle look to her face. Her aged hands were folded in her lap. A colorful lap quilt covered her legs, but I did not see her feet. She just sat there … alone … staring at the wall. I could not stop looking at her.

The magazine article I had just read reminded me of the goodness of God and His faithfulness to work all things together for good for His children. I was sitting there in that empty room, thanking God that even in that painful health situation with my husband, God was still in control and He would use it for good, eventually. We could trust God and His promises.

And then, the room was no longer empty. I stopped praying and watched her sitting there.

Often the Lord prompts me to do things or speak to people when I don't want to. "Lord, can't I just sit here and mind my own business? She doesn't seem to even know I'm here. She has not looked around the room at all."

I just keep staring at her and then I knew why … she was blind.

I sensed the Lord telling me to go to this woman and read the story to her. I argued with Him in my head: "Read the story to a perfect stranger?" I did not want to, but I was miserable as I sat there so I slowly rose from my chair and moved closer to her. I introduced myself, told her I would like to read her a story if she wouldn't mind. She turned to me and gave me a big, warm smile and said she could think of nothing better than to hear a story! And so I began …

The article was short, just several pages, but inspiring. I finished and just sat there. She reached over, groping to touch me, and patted my arm. Thanking me profusely, she began telling me about the Lord and how He used suffering to bring good to her.

Her life had been difficult with many health problems. She was diabetic and yes, she lost her eyesight and both feet. She had been confined to a wheelchair for years and lived in a nursing home with no family nearby. She had outlived most of her family.

She said she became a Christian early in life. She absolutely knew she was his child and He loved her. She was never really alone. He was always there with her.

She paused and just looked away, like she was staring at something I couldn't see, and then smiled toward me.

She told me that each time she experienced a loss, God gave her something better. When she lost her eyesight, she was fearful at first, but it allowed her to keep her eyes focused on Jesus more, without all the distractions. When she lost her feet, it kept her from running around too much. Now she sits at his feet praising Him all day long. She lost most of her family, but He is her family. She longed for the day she would finally see Him face to face. She came to know the Lord deeper in her illness and He became more and more precious to her as the years went by.

She thanked me again for reading to her. She said she missed reading but she kept Jesus and His Word always in her heart. She was happy to be right where she was because He was there with her and He was enough!

Suddenly the door opened and a nurse reached for her wheelchair and rolled her into the treatment room.

I just sat there and stared at the empty corner where her wheelchair had been just moments before. I was immersed in emotions: joy, shame, gratitude, awe.

I thought God wanted me to bless her—she blessed me.

I felt sorry for her—but sorry me, I was shallow and selfish.

Once again, thinking it was about me … it NEVER is! It is always about God and His glory. We get in it when we see Him at work!

As I read to her the story of our faithful God and His promises, He displayed one of His beautiful masterpieces! This little woman, old, blind and crippled, and I didn't even know her name!

But I was blessed to see her looking at HIM! The view was amazing!

Gratitude to God is beautiful, especially when it glows in the dark places of life.

I can still hear her little voice praising Him and see her blind eyes looking at the beauty of the invisible God she knew and loved so well! She was blind but she saw; she was trapped in the wheelchair, but she was dancing in heaven on the streets of gold!

She was here, but she was THERE!

She made me remember a poem I read once:

"The Blessing of Unanswered Prayers"
Unknown Confederate Soldier

I asked God for strength that I might achieve;
I was made weak, that I might learn humbly to obey.
I asked for health, that I might do great things;
I was given infirmity that I might do better things.
I asked for riches that I might be happy;

I was given poverty, that I might be wise.
I asked for power, that I might have the praise of men;
I was given weakness, that I might feel the need of God.
I asked for things, that I might enjoy life;
I was given life, that I might enjoy all things.
I got nothing I asked for; but everything I had hoped for.
Almost despite myself, my unspoken prayers were answered;
I am, among men, most richly blessed!

45
A Celebration of Life

IT WAS A cool, crisp October morning when I walked into the room where my friend Ethel Forrest lay. Not knowing what to expect, I slowly entered the room and looked around. The hospital bed was set up in the family room facing a large set of windows.

They lived in a beautiful home nestled on a serene bay of water in a sleepy little southern Florida town. It was an unusually gorgeous autumn day, and the view from the window was breathtakingly beautiful. Crystal clear blue waters, full billowing clouds and sunshine aglow, with the kind of warmth that goes right through you, warming your very soul. What a day!

As I peeked around the corner, there she was. Her tiny body, so fragile and still, I thought she was asleep. As I edged my way closer to her bedside, I heard her voice say, "Hello, friend!"

To my surprise, she flashed a big smile and bid me to come and sit by her side. Her silver hair, neatly coifed, her fresh powdered face, and her lipstick glowing with a delicate rosy pink surprised me. She looked like a porcelain doll. She chuckled. Did we expect her not to put on her makeup? I laughed with her and hoped I might be the same, if I ever followed in her path.

My friend had cancer. She was nearing the end of a long and courageous battle with the dreaded disease. We had become pen pals over the last several years. Being "old ladies" as such, we enjoyed the old timer's way of communication: letter writing. We were not so savvy in the email generation and loved the surprise of getting letters in our mailbox. I had grown to love this lady as we shared so many things through our letters. She was a woman who loved well, and I had come to love her dearly. She was my friend and I, hers.

Her devoted husband of many years sat at the foot of her bed, looking lost and helpless. Her three grown daughters, laden with pain and anguish, held her hands and softly cried. The pastor of her church asked if she would like us to sing for her and she said, "Yes, I'd like that." Hand in hand we gathered around her bed and began a melody of praise and worship. She joined in with each verse, although her voice was weak and frail.

We began to recite the 23rd Psalm: "The Lord is my Shepherd, I shall not want ... Yea, though I walk through the valley of the shadow of death; I will fear no evil, for Thou art with me." Verse by verse we proclaimed God's Word. At the end, she spoke so clear and calm: "I feel like I am the little lamb, and He is coming to take me home." The room seemed to take on a heavenly glow of peace and joy in the midst of pain and heartbreak. How could that be? It was, as the scripture tells us, "the peace that passeth understanding."

My friend, she knew Jesus and Jesus knew my friend. He knew her by name. "My sheep hear my voice and they follow me" (John 10:27). He was leading her home, she was following, and He was her peace.

It has been several years since my friend left to be with Jesus. Her devoted husband also passed away not long after my friend and left their three daughters abruptly orphaned.

As we journey through this life, so much of it is devastatingly painful and we can't help but question, "Why must it be so?" The Bible is very clear that this life has much tribulation, but there are facets of the beauty of God's presence that can only been seen in the dark places. All of life is to proclaim the glory and goodness of God. He is greater than the darkness and sweeter than the pain. My friend knew that and she became the example of that glow of peace. Her Savior was enough, and He carried her through her journey of cancer. I say "through" because He carried her through it, through the valley of the shadow of death into the life. The Bible says that "to be absent from the body is to be present with the Lord" (2 Corinthians 5:8)—that is the reality of life eternally with God.

My friend was a great example of a devoted wife, a loving and wonderful mother and a good friend, but most of all, she was an example of how to die. Isn't that what most good, godly mothers want to be? An example for their children to follow? We love our children from the moment we find out we are pregnant and we want to lead them in the right paths so that when we are gone, we know they will be alright.

Good mothers teach us how to live and then, if we are privileged, they show us how to die to live again.

With my friend, and with all of us who are Christians, the way is always the same … it is Jesus. He is our Savior, our strength, our hope, our joy, our peace and our Shepherd, who will carry us home to live eternally with our Heavenly Father.

Today I remember you, my friend, and I celebrate your life!

I thank God that you were my friend! I will see you again one day because of our blessed hope. Christ in us, our hope of glory!

We miss you.

46
What the Sea Has for Me

MY HUSBAND LOVES to surprise me! Taking up a silent stance in a dark room, sneaking up on me unaware, grabbing me with a shout sends him into hysterics! Shrieking, shaking, I explode into panic, shouting, "Why do you do this to me?"

Of course, after all these years, I know WHY he does it. He likes to see me startled! He thinks it's funny! I guess no matter how old men get, they are still little boys at heart, scaring little girls!

But sometimes those surprises are "altogether lovely" and I am living one of those right now!

My recently retired husband darted into our house calling his recently retired wife, "Come with me, I need to show you something and ask your advice." So, being the dutiful wife that I am (ha), I dropped everything to follow his lead and jumped into our truck.

After a few minutes of driving, my feminine curiosity could take it no more, so I asked, "Where are we going? What do you want to show me? For what do you need my advice?"

In his all too familiar answer, he replied, "You'll just have to wait," a task he knows is almost impossible when my curiosity has been piqued.

But wait I did. Several minutes passed and I noticed we had taken a turn leading us toward Perdido Key Beach. Pulling into a parking lot in front of the Sandy Key Condominium, I was about to explode with excitement! I kept asking, "Why are we here? What's going on?" Ignoring me, he went into the main office. Following him, I noticed the front desk clerk was handing him several keys. Turning, he gave me a big smile and said yes, we were going to have a little vacation at the beach! Yahoo! The question was, did we want a two-bedroom or a three-bedroom condo? He wanted me to look and then make the decision of what I wanted. What a guy! Settling on the two-bedroom, since it was right in front of the heated pool, he closed the deal. The two-bedroom it was!

After a few more weeks of waiting, the time finally came for us to move over to the beach. We were staying a whole month! I was very excited!

It's been really fun! We have shared our little piece of heaven with some family members and several of our closest friends. We have enjoyed good food, good fellowship, good sleeping and lots of laughs! It's been great! But the one thing I have enjoyed the most is my daily walks on the beach.

I am an early riser. I started waking early over 30 years ago to have my alone time with God, and dawn is my favorite part of the day. Being alone on the beach, watching the sun come up over crystal-blue waters is overwhelming to me. Absolutely breathtaking!

We have been here almost a month now and each day that I walk the beach, it's different! Some days the waves are full and angry, crashing hard into the shore. Other days it's like glass, calm and still with sunlight dancing like magical diamonds on the glistening azure blue waters. But each day the rolling waves rush to me, spilling treasures at my feet.

Shells, beautiful shells. And I search ...

You can spot the searchers, the early-rising senior citizens, on the beach. Some are snowbirds from the north who came to Florida to escape their cold weather and snow. But we all look alike on the beach early in the morning. Our gait slow, we stop frequently, staring out over the water, bending down, searching, always searching for the perfect shell. Passing each other we all have our little plastic bags of shells or bulging pockets full of our finds from the morning. We smile, we talk about how gorgeous the weather is and how we're glad it's not snowing, all the while holding on to our little trinkets from the sea.

I am from Florida. I grew up there. I can go to the beach anytime I want. Why am I searching for shells every day? Why is my plastic Ziploc bag full of sandy little treasures?

Every day on the beach I am reminded in a very concrete way that God is sovereign over all His works. That life is always moving, changing. Each little shell that finds itself on this sandy shore, at the end of its existence, is still known by the God that created it. God gave it its beginning and knew its end.

I look at the beautiful snow-white sands that we enjoy and am reminded that His children are as many as the sands of the sea and He knows each one of us. Each particle of sand, each delicate little shell all known by the God of all creation. In my finite smallness, I am overwhelmed by the infinite God. I also, a little temporary piece of dust, am known and loved by God.

Amazing grace!

So I search. I bend down and pick up my little treasures from the sea. I will take them home, place them in a clear glass container, put them on my back porch and look at them every so often. A glass full of memories … I will see them and remember this time here on the beach at Sandy Key.

Memories of a husband with wonderful surprises, full of love. Memories of fishing with grandchildren, laughing and reminiscing with old friends. Good home-cooked dinners with favorite recipes and delicious restaurant meals. Laughing and swimming in a heated pool in 35-degree weather, watching too much TV, playing games, sleeping late then cooking big hefty breakfasts, then daily walks alone on the beach searching for treasures from the sea!

Overflowing with gratitude … living life, loving others, seeing and savoring God everywhere! Thank you, Lord! You are amazing!

"Shout joyfully to God, all the earth. Sing the glory due His Name; Make His praise glorious. Say to God, 'How awesome are thy works'" (Psalm 66:1-3).

47
Beach Balls

THE LIME GREEN and white beach ball floated effortlessly on the crystal-blue water of the pool in our backyard. There were actually several different beach balls floating around, reminiscent of grandchildren who recently played there and forgot to put away all their toys.

It was an early morning in September. There was a cool autumn breeze on my back porch as I began my daily habit of Bible reading and prayer with the Lord.

I love the solitude in our backyard. Softly I began to sing and praise the Lord as I watched the beach balls glide on the top of the water. I began praying for my family members, my children, my grandchildren and others, but I couldn't keep my eyes off one of the beach balls.

The lime green one had two faces on it. One of the grandchildren probably picked it out because it was funny. One side had a big smiley face and the other side, a frown. Each time the wind shifted slightly, I saw another face. A smile … then a frown. A smile … then a frown.

I wondered, as I sat there with Bible in hand, "Am I like that to you, O Blessed Lord? When the winds shift, do I show you a different face? If the winds of adversity blow on my days, do I whine and complain and show you a frowning face?"

I rested my Bible in my lap and just watched the floating balls. How different was the ordinary multicolored striped beach ball? I watched it, the typical red, yellow, blue and white beach ball. The same breeze would spin it, but as I watched, I saw beauty instead.

Something miraculous happened to the multicolored beach ball as it turned and twisted on the pool water, as it danced with the wind. The colors began to twirl together and blend into something that looked like peppermint candy!

I found myself drawn to the twirling ball and began thinking, "Lord, how does my faith look to others as your winds touch my life? Do I live as the smile-frown or as swirling peppermint?"

Looking again into his Word, He reminded me that He is working all things together for good, even though the working out of it may not feel pleasant at the moment. His providence may come in the winds of adversity to move me away from my pride and self-sufficiency and closer to Him. His sovereign hand extends goodness to me that changes me from the inside out. He has promised to make me look more like Him as I learn to let go and surrender to His perfect will, whatever that may be.

I think in my Christian journey I've wanted the Lord to sprinkle His character on me like powdered sugar, but often I have found that real spiritual maturity has been more like being in a hurricane! He has used the winds of adversity to blow away the parts of me that are not like Him.

The hurricane puts you in helplessness. It makes you face

a power greater than yourself. It confronts you to actually see that all your positive affirmations or your own wisdom doesn't stand a chance in stopping it. Hurricanes contain terrible winds that can strip away everything you thought was solid and firm. It can all be gone in a second. If you humble yourself, bow down and pray to the One who creates the wind and the rain, then you may see Him and come to know Him in a way you have not known before … and you change.

You look different to others because you are.

Staring at the beach balls again, I wondered how long they would last. With all our grandchildren in our pool so often, plastic toys don't last very long. They are fun for a while, but they get holes in them and then they get thrown away to be replaced by another cheap little rubber toy.

I don't want to forget that morning in September when I watched the beauty of the twirling peppermint beach ball.

Ultimately, I too will be gone one day. I prayed, "Lord, let me live always surrendered to Your will. Help me to have my eyes fixed on You in happy times and in the hurricanes. You are the Sovereign God and always worthy to be praised. You are always greater then 'this,' whatever this is!"

"Hear the word of the Lord, you who tremble at His word" (Isaiah 66:5).

"The voice of Your thunder was in the whirlwind; the lightning lit up the world; the earth trembled and shook" (Psalm 7:18).

"Thus said the Lord; let not the wise man glory in his wisdom, let not mighty man glory in his might, let not the rich man glory in his riches; but let him who glories, glory in this; that he understands and

knows Me, that I am the Lord exercising lovingkindness, judgement and righteousness in the earth. For in these I delight, says the Lord" (Jeremiah 9:23-24).

"And we know that all things work together for good to those who love God to those who are the called according to His purpose. For whom He foreknew, He also predestined to be conformed to the image of His Son that He might be the firstborn among many brethren. Moreover, whom He predestined these He also called; whom He called, these He also justified; and whom He justified, these He also glorified" (Romans 8:28-30).

"Oh the depth of the riches both of the wisdom and knowledge of God! How unsearchable are His judgments and His ways past finding out! For who has known the mind of the Lord? Or who has become His counselor? Or who has first given to Him and it shall be repaid to him? For of Him and through Him and to Him are all things, to Whom be the glory forever. Amen" (Romans 11:33-36).

48
The Sound of Silence

SILENCE HAS A sound to it. It is a paradox for sure, but it's real, like the hush you feel while walking in an open field on "first" snow. The quietness is like the whisper of the Divine. It feels like a child on their mother's breast or a warm blanket on a cold day. It's comforting. Each morning, it calls to me: "Come, Thea, come to the quiet place."

My back porch is that place for me. It is usually before dawn that I come to seek solitude. I find it in our backyard. Many times, it is before daybreak. I sleepily drag my big bag full of books, turn on the light above my chaise lounge chair and slowly sip my hot coffee … and just listen. At first I hear nothing, nothing but the stillness that comforts me. I settle myself, my inward self, at the feet of my Master, the Lord Jesus Christ.

I know that I am but a puff of air, a vapor, and yet I know He knows my name for He has chosen to make me His child. His Word tells me His sheep hear His voice. So I listen. I want to hear Him … I need to hear Him.

Usually the first sound of His majesty is from one of our little feathered friends. The Bible tells me that all of nature proclaims the majesty of God. All of nature screams, "God is glorious, God is glorious!"

Here in Florida, where I live, one of the first birds to sing each morning is the mockingbird. His voice is usually the first one of the dawn. I love the voice of the mockingbird with its many different sounds. It signals the day to begin and after several choruses all alone, other birds join in the morning choir. It is a symphony of sounds in my little backyard paradise!

The sun begins to rise and then I see them all coming to greet me in my backyard. I see the blue jays, the small brown sparrows, the little titmouse with its black-and-white crowned top hat and the humble sweet doves, cooing and looking for seeds on the ground under our bird feeder. But I think my favorite is the cardinal. I love the beauty of the brilliant red and black male. He is exquisite as he perches himself on our backyard privacy fence, darting back and forth to our bird feeder.

Today I am overjoyed to see them all because for the last several months, there were no birds in our backyard! Oh, I could hear them as I would come to my place of solitude each morning, but I could only hear them in the distance. They were waking up in someone else's backyard, not ours. We had lost our backyard birds. Why?

Last summer we began a project. My husband and I decided to clear off the back lot on our property and make room to park our boat and our camper. It seemed like an easy enough project, but as most of us know, nothing is ever as simple as we think it will be. So many weeks later with much manpower and more money than we thought we would spend, the trees were all cut down and burned on a big burn pile. Our back lot was now very, very different. Our once very shady, tree-filled back lot was now hot, empty, naked and quiet ... very quiet. Of course, this was what we wanted. It was great for the storage for our boat and camper, but our bird sanctuary had become a parking lot!

We spent most of the summer traveling so we didn't notice the change, but after returning in late August, we began to feel the absence of our little bird friends. At first we thought it was because we had changed birdseed. I went to the store and purchased their favorite kind but still ... no birds. I tried blocks of peanut butter suet, but it just hung there on its chain and mildewed. We were sad.

I prayed, "Lord, please send us some birds to feed again." I never even once thought about the birds when we were chopping down all the trees!

Previously, the first bird I saw or heard every morning was the mockingbird. He would sit in a big tree in our back field that had its branches hanging over the privacy fence into our backyard. I could see him every morning from my chaise lounge as the sun came up. I am sad now as I look over there ... the tree is gone, no little gray mockingbird friend. But just because we cut down the bird sanctuary didn't mean that God quit taking care of his little birds. He just moved them elsewhere—into our neighbor's trees.

But we did not give up. We kept putting out seed and in the solitude each day, I kept praying God would once again send us some birds to feed.

One morning I saw a lone red cardinal sitting on the privacy fence singing his way into our backyard. Slowly he would swoop down to the bird feeder, taking nourishment for the day.

At first he came alone, but he came each morning for about a week. Each day I said, "Thank you, Lord." One by one I saw them come—the blue jays, the sparrows, the titmice, the doves. Slowly at first, almost hesitantly, coming to feed again at our bird feeder, here with us.

This morning I saw Mr. Cardinal chasing his young female with the mating dance of spring. They both were darting back and forth, then sitting together up in one of our palm trees by our pool. It makes me smile watching them.

Last year we also had a cardinal family in that same palm tree. I watched the mother bird make a thousand trips, her beak full of twigs and strings to build her little nest among the palms. I watched the male make his own million-mile journey, taking her seed while she worked. The male cardinal feeds the female while she builds the home for their little ones. Amazing … the beauty of God's plan for the family and for future generations!

We watched as the little eggs hatched and several baby birds appeared. I could hear them each morning, squawking for their parents to feed them. Both mom and dad seemed to be continually looking for food and carrying it up to their little ones. One day the mama bird had her little babies out on our privacy fence. They were all lined up in a row. It was flight training day. One by one she would fly out several feet from the palm tree to the fence and then back again. One by one they followed her. All but one—he just sat on the fence. He would only run back and forth on the fence while his siblings flew. Finally, he launched out, flapped his little wings and then fell. He was too small, too weak to fly. I was horrified as I watched him fall and then in an instant, the big yellow cat from next door, which had been crouched below, scooped him up and ran off! I screamed, jumped up and ran after the cat, but he scaled the fence. I couldn't catch him. I just stood there and began to cry.

I watched the frantic display of panic of both bird parents, squawking and darting back and forth from the fence to the ground and back to the palm tree again. All day long the mother bird sat on the fence. She would dart back and forth along the fence, looking down to the ground and making a woeful call. I did not see the other little birds all day. It was heartbreaking, and I cried off and on most of the day each time I looked out my kitchen window and saw her there on the back fence calling for her little one.

But the next day, life went on as usual. She continued to train her other little babies how to fly long and high. In a few days they were gone, but I think I spot them every so often, small cardinals at our bird feeder.

March is here now, and the leaves are beginning to bud on the baron fig tree in our neighbor's yard that hangs over our privacy fence. Spring, the time of new beginnings. Cardinals courting, mating, preparing for birth, then feeding, protecting, training, then releasing. The beautiful cycle of life! As you read this, I know you already know about the great cycle of life, but to see it played out in my own little backyard is spectacular! The display of God's gift of life!

The Lord says in Matthew 6:25-26, "Do not be anxious for your life, as to what you shall eat or what you shall drink nor for your body as to what you shall put on it; is not life more than food and the body for clothing? Look at the birds of the air, they do not sow, neither do they reap, nor gather into barns, and yet your Heavenly Father feeds them. Are you not worth more than them?"

And the answer is YES! Emphatically, yes!

I am worth much more than the birds, and yet as I sit here in my place of solitude each morning and watch the birds, I see how God constantly cares for them whether they are in my backyard or my neighbor's. God cares for them. When we chopped down their trees, He cared for them elsewhere. He gave them food, water, shade, twigs and strings to make their nests and gave them little ones. His loving-kindness was extended to them on their difficult days, and their beautiful days! Life goes on.

So, if you start to worry, just walk outside and look up! Find some little birds and just watch them for a while. They wake up each day not knowing where they will get their food, but God knows. He has a plan for the day … for the little birds and for us.

So do you listen for the sound of the silence? The voice of God is there. He is everywhere speaking to us. He is glorious! He is glorious! Look around, listen, watch and see! See Him in all of life around you!

"The Lord is good to all. And his mercy is over all that He has made. All Your works shall give thanks to You, O Lord, and all Your saints shall bless You! They shall speak of Your glory of Your kingdom and tell of Your power, to make known to the children of man Your mighty deeds, and the glorious splendor of Your kingdom. Your kingdom is an everlasting kingdom and Your dominion endures throughout all generations. The Lord is faithful in all His Words and kind in all His work" (Psalm 145:10).

49
Swaying Palm Trees

SITTING IN MY lawn chair in the coolness of the morning, I heard a rustling in the trees next to our privacy fence. The curious woman that I am, I got up and walked over to a very large, tall palm tree in our backyard and looked up. There were bits and pieces of flying branches falling down to the ground around my feet, which I noticed were covered with dried palm tree bark. The trunk of the palm tree had been stripped and it had a hairy brown fuzziness covering the newly exposed trunk.

Looking up again, I noticed a small gray Florida squirrel with its mouth full of the brown hairy stuff. The squirrel was dragging it up to a higher place on the palm tree and, I guess, depositing it behind some old dead palm ferns that were too high for us to get to when we trimmed the trees a few months ago. I assumed it was busy making a nest.

I just stood there and watched the squirrel as it made at least 20 trips back and forth from one tree to the next in our backyard, dragging its treasures up to the nest. Its little mouth was filled with branches and acorns and even large red pods from the magnolia trees. It was an industrious little squirrel! I hoped it was comfortable in its little nest in our tall palm tree!

I live in Florida and have always loved palm trees. There is something very relaxing and almost mystical about palms. They make you feel like you are on an island somewhere in the Caribbean sipping coconut punch, lying in a hammock, nestled between two palms swaying in the breeze. I can almost hear the steel drums and their Bob Marley music in the background.

But as much as I love palms, I had never had one in my own yard until my husband and I bought his old homestead. His father built this house himself back in the early '50s. We did a lot of remodeling to the old house, and he decided to landscape our yard.

That's when I was personally introduced to Florida palm trees, and I have come to really love them.

My husband had big dreams for our little backyard. I couldn't see it at first, but he continued to plot and plan and eventually plant and before long, he had created our own little backyard tropical paradise where we could retreat after a long day of work.

There was a comfortable covered back porch, colored landscape lighting, a small pool surrounded by almost a dozen palm trees. Of course, they were very small at first but now they are large, beautiful, majestic and almost magical!

I say "magical" because I can't believe they have survived all the storms we've had.

We live in Pensacola, Florida, hurricane alley, and we have had some doozies over the years. Hurricane Ivan was the worst, and we lost almost every tree in our front yard.

But not our backyard palm trees! Their beautiful leaves were stripped off and they were bent over, but they were not broken or ripped up at the roots—they amazingly, almost magically, survived and continued to flourish!

I actually read once that palm trees can survive almost any storm because, unlike all other trees, they only have one above-ground growing point called the "terminal bud," which is located at the top of the trunk where the ferns begin to grow. As long as that one point remains intact, the tree will continue to grow and flourish, no matter the storms that come against it.

Today I am reminded of the durability of the majestic palm tree and its continued usefulness to this little gray squirrel, another one of God's creations!

I am reminded of Psalm 92:1-3: "It is good to give thanks to the LORD, to sing praises to Your name, O Most High; to declare Your steadfast love in the morning and Your faithfulness by night. The righteous flourish like the palm tree and grow like a cedar in Lebanon. They are planted in the house of the LORD; they flourish in the courts of our God; they still bear fruit in old age; they are ever full of sap and green, to declare that the LORD is upright; He is my rock, and there is no unrighteousness in Him!"

This old, tall palm tree in my backyard is very important to this little squirrel as it builds a nest and prepares for the winter months ahead. It's just a little gray Florida squirrel, but it's also God's creation and He is supplying what the squirrel needs.

I love that. I too am just an aging little Florida woman scurrying about, but I also know I am one of God's children, made righteous because of the life, the death and the resurrection of my Savior and Master, Jesus Christ. He is my terminal bud, my source of eternal life.

So amidst the storms in my own life, the getting old and all that entails, I can rest in the fact that the righteous will continue to flourish like the palm tree because they have been planted by God into His courtyard.

Even when our old body doesn't move like it used to, our mind doesn't think like it used to, our eyes become dim and we don't see like used to, we still will bear fruit for His glory. We will still be full of the life-giving source and be green enough to continue to declare the truth of who God is!

Yes, the LORD is upright, Yes, He is my rock. Yes, there is no unrighteousness in Him, and I am forever, eternally safe in the bosom of God, our Eternal Heavenly Father, because I am in Christ, His Eternal Son.

"I love You, O LORD, my strength. The LORD is my rock and my fortress and my deliverer, my God, my rock, in whom I take refuge, my shield and the horn of my salvation, my stronghold. I call upon the LORD, who is worthy to be praised, and I am saved from my enemies. For it is You who light my lamp; the LORD, my God lightens my darkness. This God, His way is perfect; the Word of the LORD proves true; He is a shield for all those who take refuge in Him. For who is God; but the LORD? And who is a rock, except our God? The God who equipped me with strength and made my way blameless. The LORD lives, and blessed be my rock, and exalted be the God of my salvation" (Psalm 18:1-3, 28, 30-32, 46).

"If then you have been raised with Christ, seek the things that are above, where Christ is, seated at the right hand of God. Set your minds on things that are above, not on things that are on the earth. For you have died, and your life is hidden with Christ in God. When Christ,

who is your life appears, then you also will appear with Him in glory" (Colossians 3:1-4).

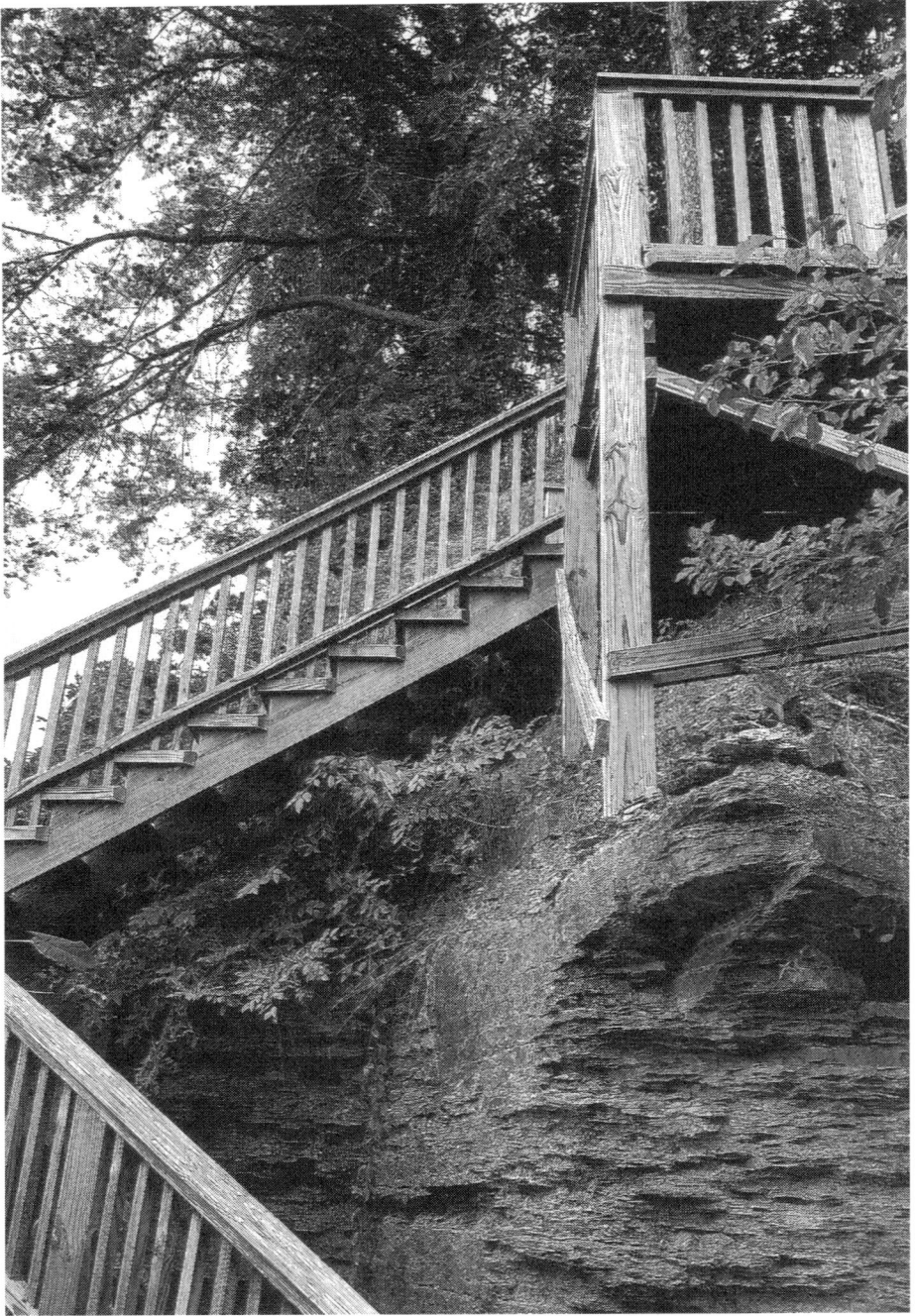

50
The Stairs to Nowhere

WANDERING AROUND IN the large backyard of my friend's lake house, I saw a raised wooden deck in the back right corner of the yard. Wooden benches lined three sides of the deck and there were several bright, colorful chairs facing the view of the lake below. It was early morning and the sun was just coming up as I walked toward the inviting deck to sit and muse awhile.

Enjoying the morning dawn, the bright-red cardinals visiting the hanging bird feeder, I just rested in the beauty of it all. Suddenly, I noticed something through the back of one of the wooden benches. It looked like a dirt path below the raised deck that I was sitting on. I got up and decided to go exploring.

The dirt path led me behind the deck in the corner of the yard to a small wooden gate. It was locked. It also was tightly wrenched with a black bungee cord to doubly ensure no entrance through the little wooden gate. But I was determined to find out where it led. With my curiosity piqued, I stooped down and began unraveling the bungee cord. I then started pushing and pulling on the gate until the lock popped open, revealing the path to somewhere.

The "somewhere" I did not know yet, but I was determined

to find out.

   Slipping through the small gate, I began the descent downward. It was really a delightful path made of weathered wood-
en 2x2s, a solid floor with handrails, a boardwalk of sorts. I began walking the boards and wondered where it would take me.

   My friend's property was on a steep hill overlooking a
lake. The descent was rather arduous. I followed along the
boardwalk for several yards; then the boardwalk turned and
went several yards in the other direction. I could tell I was on
a zigzag path but always descending downward. The view
along the way was delightful. I could see the lake below; beautiful trees and shrubs were extending out of the rocky edge of
the steep hill. I noticed the beginning of the autumn leaves of
red, yellow and gold.

   Right, then left, then down, down, down and then stop! All,
of a sudden there were no more weathered wooden stairs, just
an empty space below the last step. Cautiously I inched to the
last step. It hung over a precipice of rocks below that bordered
the lake. I was stuck! It was too high for me to jump down on
the jagged rock edge below without hurting myself. I looked
around and accepted that this was the end of my journey from
the path to somewhere. It had led me down a path to the stairs
leading to nowhere.

   Now there was nothing else to do but begin my journey
upward.

   Looking up at the stairway from where I began, I realized
I had traveled a long way down. The way up looked daunting. The sun now shining brightly on the weathered wooden
boards, their zigzag path pointed me back to the little wooden

gate behind my friend's deck.

I turned around and began the climb up: 1, 2, 3, 4 … I began to feel a slight sting in my calf muscles with each step upward … 24, 25, 26 … the tension moved up into my thighs … 58, 59, 60 … my heart began pounding a little and my breathing was labored. I kept on pushing myself, my whole body feeling the labor of the climb upward.

Finally, I could see the top. My friend's backyard was in view. I could see the little wooden gate I had pushed open. The colorful chairs were waiting for me on the deck above the little gate. I kept pushing myself with each climb up and finally squeezed through the small gate opening. I leaned down, locked it again and secured the black bungee cord. I made my way to the large deck above the path and plopped down in a bright-pink lawn chair. I felt my whole body begin to relax.

In my curiosity I had found that the stairs to somewhere actually led me down to the stairs leading to nowhere!

I wondered how many times in my life my curiosity had led me to open gates about which God had plainly said, "No, this is not good for you, Thea. Stay away from this path! It's off limits!" But in my curiosity and my rebellion, I insisted on my own way and pushed past His instructions in His Word that plainly said, "No," and I said, "Yes, but I want this!"

And so in His mercy, He let me go, to have my own way. He watched me push past His boundary of the "No." How easy it was to slide down the path leading to nowhere until I hit bottom. Then there was nowhere else to go, only emptiness on every side. I tasted all the pleasures on the path of "No." At first they tasted sweet, but now they leave me sick and hungry for something that satisfies. The Sovereign God of grace knew that as He had watched me slide on my downward path; He knew I would eventually come to a dead end. But He would be there to take my hand and lead me up.

The way of "No" is easier than the climb up to God's "Yes." But He and I began. I huffed and puffed; I had to stop along the way and rest and catch my breath to gain some strength for the next leg of the journey. But I felt His hand always holding mine, patient with my weaknesses, always hearing His kind voice: "Come, Thea, come up with Me."

Resting in the pink lawn chair on the deck in my friend's backyard, I finally enjoyed the view from up high. I laughed at myself and remembered what my mother told me when I was a little girl: "You better listen to your mama, Thea; curiosity killed the cat!" To explore and to go on journeys in life are great. We learn, we grow, but wisdom comes from God as we learn to listen and heed His warnings to us from His Word.

There is safety and security, peace and joy as we learn to live within God's boundaries. Obeying His "Yes" and His "No" is wisdom from above. If we accept His wisdom, then we can avoid the stairs going nowhere and enjoy the stairs going somewhere! His Life is one of abundance!

"Trust in the Lord with all your heart and lean not to your own understanding but in all your ways submit to Him and He will make your path straight. There is a way that seems right to a man and appears straight before him but its end is the way of death. The fear of the Lord is the beginning of wisdom. Fools despise wisdom and instruction" (Proverbs 1:7; 3:5-6; 16:25).

"The thief comes only to steal and kill and destroy. I came that they may have life and have it abundantly" (John 10:10).

51
Sagging Suntans

SUN'S UP!

That's my cue ... I can finally walk the beach!

I had been up for several hours spending time with the Lord in His Word, but now I can spend time with Him out in His wonderful creation!

I love it here in south Florida during December—it's absolutely beautiful!

My sister and brother-in-law have a condo on Fort Myers Beach. They are snowbirds for the winter, but when they aren't using their condo, they allow us the joy of spending time there. Their generosity has blessed my soul with many pleasures throughout the years!

Tying my tennis shoes and walking down three flights of stairs, I unlocked the condo gate and walked out onto the white expanse of empty beach. It's glorious and very quiet, except for the ebb and flow of the waves rushing to the shoreline, spilling beautiful seashells!

I just wanted to shout at the top of my lungs, "Thank you, Lord!" Beginning my walk, I contained myself and remembered most people aren't morning people and wouldn't appreciate my loud voice of praise! So I quietly walked and prayed. I silently praised God and began to watch for His beauty and enjoy the sweetness of His presence in the stillness of the morning!

The intimacy didn't last too long before the beach was crawling with others trying to get some early-morning exercise!

Walking on a south Florida beach in the MIDDLE of the week in December has a wonderful appeal to it!

There are NO tan, ripped, hard bodies anywhere in sight!

Those kinds of bodies are still at work or in school somewhere. Only the senior citizens can walk the beach in the middle of the week in early December! It's great!

Walking along, watching the couple in front of me holding hands, I smiled! Their thin skin was weathered-looking and saggy. The backs of their legs were tattooed with varicose veins, and their thinning gray hair glistened in the early-morning sunlight! They both shared some middle-age spread, as I noticed a little "jiggle around their middles!" They laughed a few times, but mostly they were quiet and just walked together, hand in hand.

Taking my eyes off of them, I took in a deep, salty breath and enjoyed a feeling of FREEDOM … and then realized what it is!

I, too, have sagging skin tattooed by varicose veins and it doesn't matter to me in the least bit!

We were all the same on the beach that morning; nobody was trying to impress anyone else. Oh, there were the few who passed me with a body that may be a little better than the rest of us, but you just can't make yourself young again! Tight skin and ripped bodies are gone, or maybe even the realization that you never had one in the first place. To some of the better-preserved senior citizens, it still may be a faint memory, but then to others, their life of strength is totally gone. It's a miracle for them to even have the strength to walk to the shoreline! I looked up and noticed there were some who could only enjoy the view from their condo balcony.

But that day, at least, we were all here!

We were still alive, and we were on a beautiful beach in south Florida in mid-December!

I wondered about those people I passed on the beach, asking, "What are you still living for? What are you holding on to now that youth has passed and you're old?"

I'm one of them, a senior citizen, but I know what I'm holding on to, or should I say, I know the One who is holding on to me: the eternal Word of God!

CHRIST IN me, my ONLY hope of glory!

"He has not dealt with us according to our sins, nor rewarded us according to our iniquities. For as high as the heavens are above the earth, so great is His loving-kindness toward those who fear Him, as far as the east is from the west, so far has He removed our transgressions from us. Just as a father has compassion on His children, so the Lord has compassion on those who fear Him" (Psalm 103:10-13).

And do I fear Him? Yes! Every morning when I awake, I am reminded of my humanness and the frailty of my aging life. But I am also reminded in His Holy Word that He is a compassionate Father, full of loving-kindness and tender mercy, and will never, ever leave me nor forsake any of those who look to Him!

And so, as I walked the beach of south Florida in the middle of winter, I was reminded of beautiful sunrises and also aging bodies with lives that were winding down.

As I passed people on the beach, I wondered who would be gone next December …

So I prayed for each weathered face: "Have mercy, Lord, according to Your loving-kindness, have mercy. Draw them to Yourself!"

"No one can come to Me unless the Father who sent Me draws him. And I will raise him up on the last day" (John 6:44).

"But God demonstrates His love for us in that while we were still sinners, Christ died for us. There is therefore NOW NO condemnation for those who are IN CHRIST JESUS" (Romans 5:8; 8:1).

"Whom have I in heaven but Thee? And beside Thee, I desire nothing on earth" (Psalm 73:25).

52
Slow but Sure

WALKING INTO THE kitchen, I sat down on the step stool that was wedged into the pantry space at the far end of our kitchen.

My mother was standing at the kitchen sink, washing dishes and singing. She was always singing. I thought she must have known all the songs in our church songbook. She even knew all the words of all four verses! She was unaware I had slipped into her singing space, so I just sat there quietly on the stool and stared at her and listened to her voice. I was just a little girl and I didn't understand all the words to the songs she sang, but her voice always made me feel something. I can't explain it, but it was like happy and safe and loved all at the same time.

In a few minutes she turned around, surprised, and smiled. "Thea, I didn't know you were in here! Have you finished your chores?"

It was Saturday morning, and I had few chores to do before I could go outside and play. One of those chores was to shine my daddy's church shoes. It was fun. He had a little wooden box with a handle on it where he kept his shoe-shining stuff. I liked to shine my daddy's shoes because he would give me a nickel if they were really shiny. He taught me how to rub the thick black wax all around the shoes, use the big soft brush to buff them, then spit on the toe and use the soft gray cloth to rub, rub, rub until I could see my face in the tip of his shoes! It was fun, and I'd just placed them back in his dark closet against the wall.

Looking at my mother again "square in the eyes," as my daddy always said, I concentrated REALLY hard!

I dared not use the "B" word with my parents! I learned that lesson pretty early on. Some of my friends used the "B" word with their parents, and it worked great for them. Not so much for the chubby little tan girl. I dared not use that word this morning! As my mama always told me, "I am NOT your friend's mother, I am YOUR mother, and as long as you live under our roof, you will do what we say!" I hoped, because she was MY mother and had "eyes in the back of her head," as she always told me – she knew what I was thinking.

She stopped washing dishes and said, "Thea, why don't you go outside in the front yard, lay down in the grass your daddy just cut and look up for a while. Listen to the birds, smell the grass and watch the clouds. See how many animal shapes you can find up there and then come back and tell me."

Off I ran to get lost in my make-believe world of rabbits and cats and dogs trapped in the white fluffy clouds that danced in the skies over our Beach Haven home.

My mother was pretty smart about her chubby little tan girl and what was going on inside her head.

But I was getting pretty smart too, and I was learning a few things about them. Two words that always went together: BORED and WORK! Whenever I was bored, they said I was asking for work! There was always a long list of chores to be done, even for a little girl. I was slowly learning to NEVER use the "B" word with either one of my parents!

My parents made it very clear to the chubby little tan girl that they were not put here on earth to entertain me, but to love me, take care of me and raise me to be a grown-up like them who honored God. I really didn't understand what any of that meant even though I heard it all the time. I was still little, but I was learning "slow but sure," as my mama said.

Looking back at my life this past year as I've written so many of these stories, there is one thing I know for sure: my parents were teachers. Neither of them went to college to be educated as a teacher; however, their words, their relationship, their example was always one of teaching me.

Have I learned something? I have ... "slow but sure."

They were born in the early 1900s, and life was not easy for them. They worked hard and wanted to make the best possible life for their children so we could enjoy unconditional love, security and a direction toward God and His ways. One of my mother's favorite phases for parents was that they give us roots and wings—roots into the eternal things of God and then wings to fly in our own lives of faith.

How can I put into mere words what I have learned from them? It would take an eternity.

This summer, for the very first time, my big brother, sister and I, and many of our children and grandchildren, will gather together in Beach Haven for a family reunion of the "Burge offspring," as my daddy used to call us. My daddy's been gone for more than 40 years, but I can still close my eyes and see his smile. I can picture his shimmering white hair, his hazel green eyes squinting shut, as a big smile spreads across his face, look-ing lovingly at us, then looking down sweetly to my mother and saying, "Look, honey, look what we did!"

So here I am on the last page of these 52 stories of my life, and the end is just like the beginning. All of life is to teach you one thing that I learned in the arms of my mother: "God will take care of you."

But how do I get to know this God she knew so well? Pray and seek Him daily in His Word, the Bible.

Closing my senior citizen eyes, I can still hear my mother's sweet voice singing to me, "All to Jesus I surrender, all to Him I freely give; I will ever love and trust Him, in His Presence daily live."

So just do it! That's really all you can do. You're dealing with GOD! He's in charge, not you!

And at the end of the Book, He wins … He always wins!

"But God's firm foundation stands, bearing this seal: 'The Lord knows those who are His'" (2 Timothy 2:19a).

"Jesus said, 'If you abide in my Word, then you truly are My disciples'" (John 8:31).

THE BAD NEWS

"AS IT IS written, there is none righteous, no, not one" (Romans 3:10).

"For all have sinned and come short of the glory of God" (Romans 3:23).

"For we are all as an unclean thing and all our righteousness are as filthy rags and we all do fade as a leaf and our iniquities like the wind, have taken us away" (Isaiah 64:6).

"For the wages of sin is death but the gift of God is eternal life through Jesus Christ our Lord" (Romans 6:23).

THE GOOD NEWS

"BUT GOD COMMENDETH His love toward us in that, while we were yet sinners, Christ died for us. Much more then, being now justified by His blood, we shall be saved from wrath through Him, for when we were enemies, we were reconciled to God by the death of His Son, much more, being reconciled, we shall be saved by His life" (Romans 5:8-10).

"For God so loved the world that He gave His only begotten Son, that whosoever believeth in Him should not perish but have everlasting life. For God sent not His own Son into the world to condemn the world but that through Him might be saved. He that believeth on Him is not condemned but he that believeth not is condemned already because he hath not believed in the Name of the only begotten Son of God" (John 3:16-18).

"Jesus saith unto him, 'I am the way, the truth, and the life; no man cometh unto the Father, but by Me'" (John 14:6).

"And this is the record that God hath given to us eternal life and this life is in His Son. He that hath the Son hath life and He that hath not the Son of God hath not life" (1 John 5:11-12).

"But God, who is rich in mercy, for His great love wherewith He loved us, even when we were dead in sins, hath quickened us together with Christ, by grace are ye saved; and hath raised us together, and made us sit together in heavenly places in Christ Jesus; that in the ages to come He might shew the exceeding riches of his grace in His kindness toward us through Christ Jesus. For by grace are ye saved through faith; and that not of yourselves; it is the gift of God; not of works, lest any man should boast" (Ephesians 2:4-9).

THE BIG QUESTION: WHO IS JESUS TO *YOU*?

"He (Jesus) saith unto them, 'But whom say ye that I am?' And Simon Peter answered and said, 'Thou art the Christ, the Son of the living God'" (Matthew 16:15-16).

"For whosoever shall call upon the name of the Lord shall be saved" (Romans 10:13).

ABOUT THE AUTHOR

THEA J. COKER is a spiritual coach and all-around cheerleader for the Almighty. With over thirty years teaching God's Word at church groups, Thea has empowered women of all ages to grow in their faith.

Her writings focus on Biblical principles that guide everyday actions. Told with good-hearted humor and a personal touch, her stories speak to the soul of Christian theology.

Thea enjoys exploring the beauty of God's creation through painting, photography, and nature walks. She is blessed with a happy marriage to Don, a retired pastor. Together, they have five adult children and seventeen grandchildren.

If you would like to reach out to Thea or hire her for an event, she would love to hear from you at theacoker1@gmail.com.

Made in the USA
Middletown, DE
26 October 2018